MAKING
STRATEGY
WORK

MAKING STRATEGY WORK

HOW SENIOR MANAGERS PRODUCE RESULTS

Richard G. Hamermesh

Harvard Business School

JOHN WILEY & SONS
New York • Chichester • Brisbane • Toronto • Singapore

Published by John Wiley & Sons, Inc.

Library of Congress Cataloging in Publication Data:
Hamermesh, Richard G.
    Making strategy work.

    (The Wiley management series on problem solving,
decision making, and strategic thinking)
        Includes index.
        1. Strategic planning.   2. Industrial management—
Case studies.   I. Title.   II. Series.
HD30.28.H35   1985   658.4'012   85-12456
ISBN 0-471-80319-7

Printed in the United States of America

10 9 8 7 6 5 4 3 2 1

To
Lorie, Josh, and Molli

Preface

The development of this book closely parallels my academic career, which began in 1976 when I joined the business policy group at the Harvard Business School. At that time, I immediately confronted the problem of reconciling the policy course's historic focus on the tasks, functions, and responsibilities of the general manager with a new set of planning techniques—now commonly referred to as *portfolio planning*. These techniques offered logical, easy-to-understand prescriptions for the key general management tasks of allocating resources and setting divisional objectives.

Rather than dismiss portfolio planning as a fad, my pedagogic instinct was to see whether case materials could be developed that would test the underlying assumptions of portfolio planning, such as the roles of market share and growth in determining profitability and investment opportunities. The result was the development of case material and two articles published in the *Harvard Business Review* in 1978 and 1979.

As the popularity of strategic planning persisted and increased, however, I became more and more disturbed that, despite the publication of numerous articles on the theory underlying portfolio management, virtually nothing was being written on how these tools were actually used by managers and what impact they were having. It was this gap, and my curiosity about these issues, that motivated the research for this book.

Believing that the best way to understand how managers actually use the concepts of portfolio planning would be to observe and question managers directly, I embarked on a clinical investigation that brought me inside more than twenty companies and in contact with numerous executives. The result, I believe, is a study that goes beyond speculation to one that presents empirical data on how senior managers use strategic management tools to achieve corporate objectives and on the organizational consequences of the approach.

RICHARD G. HAMERMESH

Boston, Massachusetts
November 1985

Acknowledgments

Because my research has taken me into so many companies and has been reviewed over the years by so many colleagues, there are many whose contributions I would like to acknowledge. First, I want to offer my sincere thanks to the many busy executives who permitted me to study their practices and shared their experiences with me. Most of the companies that were studied are mentioned by name in the book, so I will not acknowledge all of them individually here. I would, however, like to single out the Dexter Corporation and the General Electric Company, whose executives allowed me to study them in great detail over an extended period of time. Special thanks are also extended to the ten chief executive officers who agreed to be interviewed in the last stage of the research. The interviews were time consuming and detailed, yet all the CEOs willingly and patiently answered my questions, challenged my ideas, and shared their own experiences and theories.

Many colleagues assisted in various parts of this study, and I am very indebted to each of them. Lyn Christiansen and Joe Bower helped me to understand the voluminous data available on the Memorex Corporation. Rod White assisted with much of the research for the Dexter case, and Frank Aguilar was a close collaborator at General Electric. Michelle Marram provided valuable help in locating library materials on the companies studied, and Paul Anderson played a key role in developing the financial model described in Chapter 3. Finally, very special help was provided by Rod White and Philippe Haspeslagh, who made available to me their data bases on the uses of portfolio planning.

As my work progressed from the research to the writing stage, I benefited from the comments of many colleagues and academic neighbors, including Joe Badaracco, Ned Bowman, Al Chandler, Ron Fox, Paul Lawrence, Henry Mintzberg, Tom Piper, Walt Salmon, Len Schlesinger, Dick Vancil, and Kirby Warren. The later drafts benefited immeasurably from the suggestions of Ken Andrews, Bob Eccles, Mal Salter, and Howard Stevenson. I am especially grateful to Joe Bower, who offered valuable advice on how to organize the presentation, and to Jay Lorsch, who suggested that I expand the research to include the interviews with the ten chief executive officers.

I also want to acknowledge those who helped in the production of this book in other ways. The Division of Research at the Harvard Business School, under the leadership of Richard Rosenbloom and later Raymond Corey, provided encouragement and financial support. Mary Barno, a freelance editor for the Division of Research, edited the entire manuscript and was a source of constant reassurance. Special thanks are extended to Rose Giacobbe and Aimee Hamel of the Harvard Business School's Word Processing Department for typing the manuscript and for never believing me when I promised that there would be no more revisions. Mary Ann O'Brien, my secretary, deserves special recognition for her hard work and good humor in supervising this effort and in ensuring that I arrived at the right company on the right day.

This effort would not have been completed without the encouragement and support of my wife and children. Not only were they understanding of my erratic travel and writing schedules, but they provided the useful diversions that kept this effort in perspective.

While I am grateful for all the help I received, the final product is mine, and I accept full responsibility for its errors and shortcomings.

R.G.H.

Contents

PART 2   THE PRACTICE OF PORTFOLIO PLANNING

MAKING
STRATEGY
WORK

Part 1

Theory and Concepts

1

Planning in Perspective

On May 14, 1970, Fred Borch, the chief executive officer (CEO) of the General Electric Company, was preparing to address his senior management group about some changes he wanted to make in how the company approached strategic planning. Though Borch didn't know it at the time, the changes he was about to announce not only would have a profound effect on GE but eventually would also influence the planning practices of most large, diversified American corporations. For Borch, however, the changes represented what he hoped would be the first steps in a solution to some problems that had plagued him since he became CEO in 1963.

The most immediate of Borch's problems was the profitless growth General Electric had experienced throughout the 1960s. In 1970, GE's sales were 40% higher than they had been in 1965, yet profits were slightly lower. This lackluster profit performance came at a time when three major new business ventures—commercial jet engines, mainframe computers, and nuclear power plants—were demanding more and more of the company's financial resources. Pressure on Borch and senior management was mounting: GE's "sacred Triple A bond rating" was in jeopardy. It was in response to these financial pressures that Fred Borch began to look for a new form of strategic planning.

Improving GE's financial situation and developing new planning approaches were not easy tasks. In 1970, GE was widely diversified, competing in 23 of the 26 two-digit standard industrial code categories, and the company was decentralized into 10 groups, 46 divisions, and over 190 departments. Under decentralization, the 190 departments were the basic organizational building blocks, each producing its own long-range plan and each with its own product/market scope and its own marketing, finance, engineering, manufacturing, and employee relations functions.

While decentralization had led to tremendous growth at General Electric, it presented serious difficulties for Fred Borch, who not only had to comprehend and review the plans of 190 different departments, but who also had to approve or reject the ambitious investment plans that most of these departments were proposing. On what basis was he to make these decisions when all of the departments could present convincing arguments and figures justifying investment in their business?

In an interview with me, Reginald Jones, who succeeded Borch as CEO in 1972, offered the following diagnosis of GE's problems at the time:

> Our performance reflected poor planning and a poor understanding of the businesses. A major reason for this weakness was the way we were organized. Under the existing structure with functional staff units at the corporate level, business plans received only functional reviews. They were not given a business evaluation.
>
> True, we had a corporate planning department, but they were more concerned with econometric models and environmental forecasting than with hard-headed business plan evaluation. Fortunately, Fred Borch was able to recognize the problem.

To help unravel these problems and to obtain an outside perspective, in 1969 Borch commissioned McKinsey & Company to study the effectiveness of GE's corporate staff and of the planning done at the operating level. It was the outcome of their report that Borch was about to report to his most senior managers on May 14. He told them:

They [McKinsey & Company] were totally amazed at how the company ran as well as it did with the planning that was being done or not being done at various operating levels. But they saw some tremendous opportunities for moving the company ahead if we devoted the necessary competence and time to facing up to these, as they saw it, very critical problems.

In their report, they made two specific recommendations. One was that we recognize that our departments were not really businesses. We had been saying that they were the basic building blocks of the company for many years, but they weren't. They were fractionated and they were parts of larger businesses. The thrust of the recommendation was that we reorganize the company from an operations standpoint and create what they call Strategic Business Units— the terminology stolen from a study we made back in 1957. They gave certain criteria for these, and in brief what this amounted to were reasonably self-sufficient businesses that did not meet head-on with other strategic business units in making the major management decisions necessary. They also recommended as part of this that the 33 or 35 or 40 strategic business units report directly to the CEO regardless of the size of the business or the present level in the organization.

Their second recommendation was that we face up to the fact that we were never going to get the longer-range work done that was necessary to progress the company through the '70s, unless we made a radical change in our staff components. The thrust of their recommendation was to separate out the ongoing work necessary to keep General Electric going from the work required to posture the company for the future.[1]

While McKinsey's recommendations addressed the problems of inadequate review of too many long-range plans, even with the reduction in the number of plans from 190 departments to 43 strategic business units (SBUs), Fred Borch still faced the formidable tasks of reviewing all of the plans and determining which of the SBUs should have their investment requests approved and which should be cut back. One GE manager noted that "Borch had a sense that he wasn't looking for lots of data on each business unit but really wanted 15 terribly important and significant pages of data and analysis." To meet this need GE, working in collaboration with McKinsey, developed a simple three-by-three matrix that distinguished both the growth and the profit potential of its SBUs. Depending on where an SBU was located on this matrix, Borch could make an independent judgment as to which SBUs should have their investment proposals approved.*

FOCUS AND OBJECTIVES OF THIS STUDY

The three innovations that were developed under Fred Borch's guidance at General Electric—SBUs, corporate review capability, and the matrix to differentiate resource allocation—formed the basis of a new approach to strategic planning at GE. Today these concepts are commonly referred to as *portfolio planning* or the *portfolio approach to strategic planning*, and they have come to dominate the planning practices of large American corporations.

Despite the widespread use of portfolio planning, however, today many are questioning its impact and it has become almost fashionable to criticize both planning and planners.[2] While some of this criticism is most appropriate, much of it seems to be based solely on speculation and personal opinion. For despite the many advances that have occurred in the fields of strategy and planning and the proliferation of writings on these subjects, little attention has been paid to how the supposed beneficiaries, the chief executive officers of our largest companies, actually use strategic planning to move their companies forward.

This book attempts to fill this void by studying how the CEOs of large diversified corporations use the portfolio approach to strategic planning. The opening account of how the General Electric Company became a pioneer in the use of portfolio planning illustrates my approach, in that it links the adoption of portfolio planning to the needs of GE's CEO, Fred Borch, at a particular

---

*The three-by-three matrix is described in greater detail later in this chapter. General Electric's experiences with portfolio planning from 1970 to 1984 are described in Chapter 10.

time. Borch began to develop and use what would later be called portfolio planning not because he was searching for a sophisticated planning system but because he had specific problems that needed to be solved: profitless growth, too many businesses to comprehend and review, and little control over capital allocations. Portfolio planning thus was adopted and used at GE only because it was able to provide solutions to Borch's problems. As I studied other companies (and other General Electric CEOs), my primary attention was on determining why and how their chief executives were using portfolio planning.

The book's focus on both portfolio planning and CEOs' use of this system reflects my dual objectives of providing a critical assessment of the uses of portfolio planning techniques and of developing a comprehensive view of how strategy is planned and implemented in large diversified companies. Simply put, the book examines how portfolio planning does and does not help chief executives develop total strategies for their companies.

I singled out portfolio planning for study for two major reasons. First, the approach has remained in the forefront of management practice for almost 15 years. Indeed, a recent survey of a sample of *Fortune* 1000 firms found that about half of those companies use portfolio planning as a part of their formal planning process.[3] Second, considerable controversy has arisen regarding the impact of portfolio planning. For example, in their widely read article, "Managing Our Way to Economic Decline,"[4] Hayes and Abernathy singled out portfolio planning as one of the causes of our industrial malaise, arguing that "the analytic formulas of portfolio theory push managers even further toward an extreme of caution in allocating resources." In contrast, one of the CEOs interviewed during this study gave the following endorsement of the approach:

> *Portfolio planning became relevant to me as soon as I became CEO. I was finding it very difficult to manage and understand so many different products and markets. I just grabbed at portfolio planning, because it provided me with a way to organize my thinking about our businesses and the resource allocation issues facing the*

total company. I became and still am very enthusiastic. I guess you
could say that I went for it hook, line, and sinker.

While this book will provide a critical assessment of the uses
and impact of portfolio planning, it does not join the debate about
the theory that underlies the portfolio approach.[5] Instead it presents the theory of portfolio planning as having a great deal of
relevance to the problems facing CEOs in large diversified companies, as evidenced by its widespread use. The book does focus
its attention on how the theory is actually applied, what problems
or issues arise from its use, and the extent to which it helps CEOs
to develop and implement comprehensive strategies.

The perspective of the CEO is taken for several reasons. First, as
illustrated in the General Electric example, the theory underlying
portfolio planning directly addresses the problems that CEOs face
in allocating resources to a group of semiautonomous and diverse
businesses. Equally important, the CEO's perspective enables us
to examine the purposes for which portfolio planning is being
used and how it relates to the other ways CEOs ensure the successful development and implementation of strategy. Chief executives are concerned with much more than analytic techniques and
planning theories. They are also concerned that the managers of
their many businesses are capable of formulating appropriate
strategies and that these managers can then effectively implement
those strategies. The CEO's perspective, then, facilitates a focus
on the relationship between portfolio planning and the entire
process of creating and implementing strategy.

With these objectives and perspectives in mind, I have had
three sets of questions guiding the inquiry:

1. **Why have CEOs adopted portfolio planning techniques?**
   How have they used portfolio planning to help them accomplish their goals? What different uses do CEOs make of
   portfolio planning? What causes this variation?

2. **What issues do companies face when using the portfolio
   approach?** What are its positive and negative organiza-

tional consequences? What impact does it have on the processes by which strategies are formulated and implemented?

3. **What impact have portfolio planning techniques had on the strategies companies have adopted?**   Which strategic decisions are most positively and negatively affected? Has portfolio planning contributed to the decline in the competitiveness of U.S. companies?

Before turning to the research that I undertook to answer these questions and to an overview of the findings, the meaning of the portfolio approach to strategic planning and how this approach relates to the problems of the CEO must be clarified. The rest of the book will then deal with the use of portfolio planning and with the application of the theory.*

THE THEORY OF PORTFOLIO PLANNING

The portfolio approach to strategic planning was first developed in the late 1960s in work done independently at the Boston Consulting Group, at McKinsey & Company, and at the Strategic Planning Institute.[†] Today numerous other consulting firms and academics have developed their own versions of portfolio planning.[6] While these different versions can lead to very different classifications of a company's businesses, on a conceptual level the similarities among them are more noteworthy than their differences.[7] As Bettis and Hall have concluded:

*Readers already familiar with portfolio planning techniques can skip the next section and continue on page 19.

†The work that led to the founding of the Strategic Planning Institute was originally done at the Marketing Sciences Institute as its PIMS (Profit Impact of Marketing Strategies) program. The success of the PIMS program eventually led to its spin-off as the separate Strategic Planning Institute.

> *Regardless of the particular layout for the matrix, the basic idea behind the portfolio concept remains the same: the position (or box) that a business unit occupies within the matrix should determine the strategic mission and the general characteristics of the strategy for the business.*[8]

In this study, the portfolio approach to strategic planning is defined as *those analytic techniques that aid in the classification of a firm's businesses for resource allocation purposes and for selecting a competitive strategy on the basis of the growth potential of each business and of the financial resources that will be either consumed or produced by the business.* While numerous portfolio planning approaches exist, only four of the most commonly used are considered here. In addition, the experience curve will be discussed because the theory underlying it was so instrumental in the development of portfolio planning.

The Experience Curve

The experience curve was conceived by the Boston Consulting Group. Conceptually it is closely related to the learning curves that were first identified in the aircraft-manufacturing industry, where it was observed that the manufacturing costs of a particular airplane fell as more aircraft were produced.[9] The underlying reason for this decline in costs was that, as greater volumes of a particular product were produced, workers and management learned to produce the product more efficiently. Hence the term *learning curve.*

The experience curve differs from the learning curve in that it applies to all costs. The hypothesized relationship underlying the experience curve is that average total costs will decline as the accumulated experience associated with selling, producing, engineering, and financing that product increases. In numerous industries, it has been shown that average total costs per unit (in constant dollars) have declined at a predictable rate with each doubling of accumulated production. Figure 1.1 shows the experience curves for two separate products. The different slopes of the

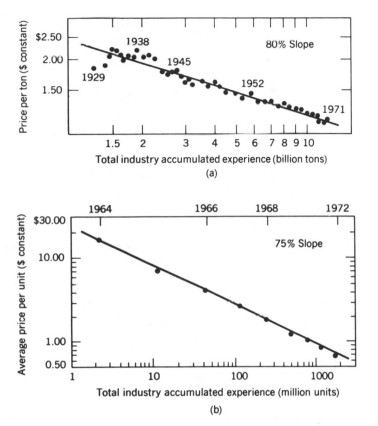

Figure 1.1. Comparison of experience curves for two products. (a) Crushed and broken limestone. Data from U.S. Bureau of Mines. (b) Integrated circuits. Data published by Electronics Industry Association. Slopes show that costs of integrated circuits declined more rapidly with accumulated experience than did costs of crushed limestone.

curves indicate that the costs of one of the products declined more rapidly with accumulated experience than was the case with the other.[10]

Although experience curves have been derived for numerous products, the reasons for the underlying relationship are not understood precisely. Among the most commonly cited are economies of scale in manufacturing, marketing, engineering, and financing; labor efficiencies; product standardization; and process improvements. The strategic implications of the learning curve are clearer—the company with the most accumulated experience can have the lowest costs, and therefore a company should invest rapidly and early to accumulate experience.

The Growth-Share Matrix

The growth-share matrix is a logical extension of the experience curve relationship. Its major contribution has been the conceptualization of a company as a portfolio of businesses that can be classified according to their potential for cash generation or cash usage.[11]

The growth-share matrix uses market share as a proxy for accumulated experience. In theory, when competitors can exploit similar experience curves, the company with the highest market share will have the greatest accumulated experience and the lowest costs. With lower costs, high market share businesses should be more profitable and thus should generate more cash than businesses with a smaller market share. Thus market share is one axis of the growth-share matrix and is a proxy for the cash-generation potential of a business.

The other axis of the growth-share matrix is market growth, which predicts the cash usage of a business. Here the posited relationship is that a rapidly growing business, with its attendant needs for new plants, equipment, and working capital, will require cash to finance its growth.

Combining market share and market growth has led to the development of the growth-share matrix shown in Figure 1.2. The matrix is divided into four quadrants with the following *hypothesized* characteristics:

High Share/High Growth. These businesses are in the most advantageous positions, such as those enjoyed by IBM in mainframe computers and Southland Corporation (7-Eleven stores) in retailing. They require heavy investments to sustain their growth, but their high market shares provide high profits to finance expansion. As a result, these businesses often produce

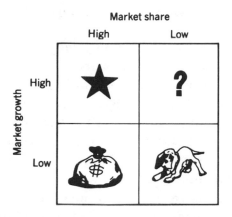

Figure 1.2. Growth-share matrix. A business with a high market share and a high growth rate is a "star"; one with a high market share but a low growth rate is a "cash cow"; one with a low market share but a high growth rate is a "question mark"; and a business low in both factors might be called a "dog."

as much cash as they consume. Such businesses are often termed *stars.*

High Share/Low Growth.   With their high share, these businesses produce large profits and cash flow. But because their industries aren't growing rapidly, there is little need to reinvest the profits for expansion. These businesses produce a large positive cash flow; they are frequently labeled *cash cows.* An example would be the leading department store in a slowly growing metropolitan area.

Low Share/High Growth.   Because they compete in rapidly growing markets, these businesses require large amounts of cash to finance growth. But their low market share and hence low profitability means that the business does not generate much cash. These businesses are often referred to as *question marks, wildcats,* or *problem children.*

Low Share/Low Growth.   These businesses do not require much investment but also do not produce much cash flow. Overall they tend to use modest amounts of cash and are commonly labeled *dogs.*

The Company Position/Industry Attractiveness Screen

Another technique for classifying businesses is the company position/industry attractiveness screen that was developed by McKinsey & Company in conjunction with the General Electric Company as described at the beginning of the chapter.[12]

The company position/industry attractiveness screen is similar to the growth-share matrix with some subtle yet important differences. As can be seen in Figure 1.3, the two axes in this matrix are industry attractiveness and company position. Industry attractiveness includes market growth, as in the growth-share matrix, but also reflects such considerations as industry profitability, size, and pricing practices. Similarly, company position includes market share as well as technologic position, profitability, and size, among others. Finally, the company position/industry attractiveness screen is usually displayed as a three-by-three matrix, often referred to as a nine-block matrix.

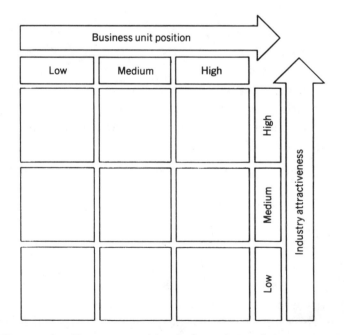

Figure 1.3.   Company position industry/attractiveness screen

Both matrices seek to categorize a company's cash flow position. However, the company position/industry attractiveness screen, which has a number of variables that must be factored into a single measure, is generally a more subjective tool than the growth-share matrix, a feature that its adherents applaud and its critics deride.

Strategic Mandates

The portfolio planning techniques just described can be used for classifying a firm's businesses on the basis of their tendency to produce or to consume cash. These techniques can also be used for selecting a strategic mandate or basic, overall objective for the competitive strategy of a business.

If one accepts the assumptions that large corporations attempt to finance their growth from internally generated cash flow and debt* and that most markets eventually reach a mature state of slow growth, strategic mandates can be specified for each category of business. In the growth-share classification, the following strategic mandates are prescribed:

Stars should receive their full share of capital and should be encouraged to invest capital to grow and maintain their strong market share positions.

Cash cows should be suppliers of cash to other businesses (stars and question marks). Investment in them should be minimized, to maximize their cash flow.

Question marks should be invested in, to improve their market share. Given the large amounts of capital required to move a question mark into the star category, however, most corporations can afford to support only a limited number of question marks.

---

*This assumption is generally a valid one and is discussed in greater detail in Chapter 3.

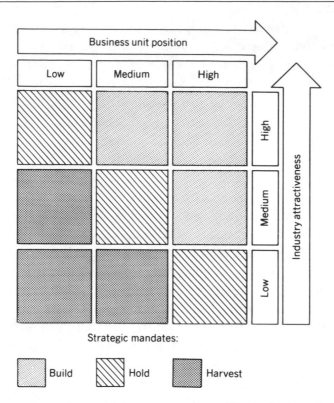

Figure 1.4. Strategic mandates: company position/industry attractiveness screen

Dogs should be divested. With their low profitability and low growth potential, dogs are considered cash traps. Resources should not be squandered on them.

The strategic mandates for a firm using the company position/ industry attractiveness matrix are similar and are shown in Figure 1.4. In both approaches, the purpose of the strategic mandates is to create a pattern of capital spending whereby a business receives funding early in its life so that it achieves a strong (i.e., profitable) competitive position. Then, as its market matures, the business will produce the cash flow that will fund other, more rapidly growing businesses. Significantly, the strategic mandates also facilitate the creation of a portfolio of businesses in which the sources and uses of funds are nearly balanced.

The PIMS Approach

On the basis of an analysis of a data base containing information on the characteristics of more than 1000 separate businesses, several PIMS (profit impact of marketing strategies) models have been developed that are an additional portfolio planning tool.[13]

The best known of these is the PAR report, which compares the profitability (return on investment, or ROI) of a particular business with that of the other businesses in the PIMS data base. It then determines whether the ROI of the business in question is greater or less than that of other businesses that are in similar circumstances. The underlying logic of the PAR report is rooted in an equation that determines ROI on the basis of about 30 variables. After quantification of these 30 variables for a particular business, a PAR report can be generated (Figure 1.5, on page 18).

Although several PIMS models produce reports that provide strategic mandates, for our purposes we can simply note that investment is encouraged in those businesses whose actual and PAR ROI are high. In other words, if a business has the characteristics of high return businesses and is indeed earning high returns, it should be fully funded. On the other hand, if a business's ROI is low but its PAR is also low, there is little reason to expect much improvement in ROI, and subsequent investment is discouraged.

THE CHIEF EXECUTIVE'S PROBLEM AND PORTFOLIO PLANNING

The previous discussion highlights the major features of the *theory* of portfolio planning. This theory has been the subject of considerable investigation as researchers have collected data and debated the existence of the experience curve and the characteristics of businesses with different market shares and growth rates.[14] Yet despite these debates, portfolio planning has persisted as one of the most widely used planning techniques in diversified corporations. This level of acceptance can be explained not because the

Category	Impact on PAR ROI (pretax)%
Attractiveness of business environment	0.6
Strength of your competitive position	1.9
Differentiation of competitive position	4.1
Effectiveness of use of investment	4.5
Discretionary budget allocation	5.4
Company factors	0.2
Change, action factors	0.5
Total impact	17.2
Average ROI, all PIMS businesses	16.7
PAR ROI, Business 12345	33.9%

Figure 1.5. PAR report. ROI: return on investment; PIMS: profit impact of marketing strategies. The average PIMS business has an ROI of 16.7%. Business 12345 has an ROI of 33.9%. The PAR report explains that only 0.6 percentage point of the business's superior performance is attributable to the attractiveness of its business environment. Most of the superior performance can be attributed to the effective use of investment and discretionary spending to achieve a differentiated position.

entire theory of portfolio planning is beyond question, but because certain key parts of the theory are responsive to one of the major problems facing chief executives of large diversified companies: the allocation of resources. Reginald Jones described this benefit of portfolio planning as follows:

> You see, regardless of the size of a company, no company can afford everything it would like to do. Resources have to be allocated. The essence of strategic planning is to allocate resources to those areas that have the greatest future potential. This is what

General Electric had been lacking and what portfolio planning provided us with.

Appreciation of why resource allocation is such a major problem for diversified companies requires an understanding of the nature of these companies and of the limits of traditional capital budgeting procedures.

Today the two most distinctive features of large industrial corporations are their diversity and their multiple levels of general management. Whereas in 1949 about one third of the *Fortune* 500 companies derived over 95% of their sales from a single business, today fewer than 5% can be classified as competing in a single business.[15] The decline of the single business company has been accompanied by the growth of the diversified firm. Whether it be DuPont competing in related businesses derived from its research into chemistry, or a conglomerate such as Textron, or United States Steel acquiring Marathon, the result has been the emergence of the diversified corporation as the dominant group among the United States' largest enterprises.

Management of diversified companies nearly always requires multiple levels of general managers. For example, in many diversified companies, reporting to the CEO are two executive vice presidents, who in turn have several group vice presidents reporting to them, who in turn have several division general managers reporting to them. These multiple levels of general management are supposed to provide closer contact and supervision of the many diverse businesses than the CEO could provide alone.

For the chief executive of these companies, however, this high level of diversity and the multilevel structure can seriously complicate the seemingly straightforward task of assuring that resources are allocated to those divisions with the best prospects for profitable growth. This is because of the difficulty the CEO has in comprehending all of the competitive forces at play in numerous diversified markets, and because of the tendency for all of the levels in the management hierarchy to support projects emanating from their divisions. The typical result is what Fred Borch and

Reginald Jones experienced at General Electric: more projects, receiving the strong backing of many managers, than the company can afford to fund.

Prior to the development of portfolio planning, capital budgeting procedures (in which all investment proposals with an internal rate of return higher than the hurdle rate are approved) were supposed to assure efficient resource allocation. These procedures, however, are by themselves inadequate, because in practice the managers making the proposals see to it that virtually all capital requests clear the hurdle rate. Moreover the requests do not all arrive at the same time, so their ranking or comparison is virtually impossible. Finally the requests are enthusiastically backed by the responsible general managers, who have considerably greater understanding of the project than does the CEO.[16]

In his path-breaking study of the resource allocation process, Bower concluded that the way to overcome the limitations of traditional capital budgeting procedures is to link the approval of specific projects to the approval of a division's entire strategic plan:

> *The process of committing the corporation to a market and products, and the process of expressing that commitment in concrete and machinery, are critically interdependent. The quality of the decisions made depends upon the identical set of market analyses and forecasts.*[17]

Significantly, the theory of portfolio planning addresses many of the difficulties CEOs face in allocating resources by taking attention away from individual investment requests and instead linking decisions about such requests to the competitive performance of the divisions and to their strategic plans. The first way this is accomplished, as we saw at General Electric, is by conceiving of the company as a portfolio of businesses. Because each of these businesses competes in a different market, each business's performance can be measured within its market. Resource allocation decisions can then be made on the basis of competitive performance, rather than by mere evaluation of investment requests.

The theory of portfolio planning also links business and investment planning, because portfolio planning focuses on each business's overall need for investment or its ability to generate cash. In practice, this is accomplished by use of strategic mandates and business classification matrices that indicate the extent to which each business, rather than each specific project, should be funded. Each investment project is still subject to a review process, but rather than focusing solely on the internal rate of return of the particular project, portfolio planning considers whether the business proposing the project should be funded in the first place. Thus when a business is classified as a star, not only is the explicit statement made that the business strategy should include growth as a central objective, but the implicit assumption is that the business will receive the investment funds it needs to grow. Similarly, a strategy to hold market share goes hand in hand with the resource allocation choice to take cash away from the business in question.

While chief executives may have difficulty telling some of their division managers that the division will not be receiving much new investment, portfolio planning theory points to the necessity of this, so that other businesses with better prospects can be fully funded. This is because one of the major implications of the experience curve is that if management does not invest aggressively and manage in ways that bring costs down or that make technologic breakthroughs in its strong businesses, it risks losing its advantage in those businesses to competitors that do. Significantly, it is this tough-minded approach toward weaker businesses that enables CEOs to use portfolio planning, as Fred Borch and Reg Jones have done, to control resource allocation and to ensure that businesses with the greatest future potential are fully funded.

THE USE OF PORTFOLIO PLANNING

While the theory of portfolio planning addresses the resource allocation problem facing CEOs of diversified companies, the theory by itself does not account for other uses CEOs have made of the techniques. For example, one chief executive told me that he did not use portfolio planning as a tool to allocate resources but rather as a way to "confront divisional management with information that forces them to think strategically." Another CEO commented that the usefulness of portfolio planning had been limited to suggesting how the company should be reorganized. Another stated that he used the techniques because they provided "a way of thinking about and understanding our businesses and of generating the agenda of what we have to do." Clearly, when we turn from the theory to the actual use of portfolio planning, we find that chief executives have been able to relate the techniques to their needs in a variety of ways. While these needs and uses are described in detail in Chapter 4, here it is important to acknowledge that one of the major reasons for the persistence of portfolio planning is that it can be used for multiple purposes.

Not only does the theory underlying portfolio planning not predict its various uses but it also offers no advice on how it should be used and what impact the techniques are likely to have. Indeed as soon as our attention shifts from theory to practice, a number of questions come to mind:

1. How should the different businesses in a company be defined?
2. What is the impact on a business of designating its role in the corporate portfolio?
3. What administrative problems accompany the use of portfolio planning techniques?
4. Are portfolio planning techniques used in different ways? If so, how and why?

Answering questions such as these and the ones listed at the beginning of this chapter, and identifying the multiple uses of portfolio planning, require documentation of the experiences companies have had in using the techniques. Such documentation will not provide conclusive evidence that all companies use the techniques in certain ways, but it can suggest the ways the techniques are used and the range of benefits and problems that can result from their use. The research undertaken for this book was thus designed specifically to provide examples of how portfolio planning techniques have been and are being used and what impact the techniques have on strategic processes and decisions.

The first phase of the research was a series of about one-day interviews with executives at each of six companies. This was followed by interviews with 20 senior executives attending Harvard's Advanced Management Program. These discussions suggested that, although portfolio planning techniques were having a marked impact, their impact and use differed significantly from company to company and over time. The following comments made by executives at four different companies are typical:

> We have been pretty aggressive in our use of these techniques. But we do not assign our businesses to categories. That is too loaded and can lead to poor decisions.

> These tools have been more helpful at the corporate level, where they help us to understand our businesses better. But the division general managers remain skeptical. They say it would be dangerous to make their strategies too explicit.

> At first, when we were doing a lot of divestitures, we used the techniques a lot. Now that the divestitures have stopped, portfolio planning isn't as visible.

> Our experience with these techniques is that they are too focused on strategy rather than decisions. We are changing our approach to highlight the major decisions each of our businesses will be facing in the future.

The initial interviews did not explain the reasons for the differences in use of portfolio planning or exactly what impact portfolio planning was having. These could be determined only by detailed observation of companies and interviews with numerous organization members at various levels. The perspective of the CEO also had to be included, obtained from the CEO directly and from data on the processes by which strategies were formulated and implemented. These requirements had to be met if this study was to reveal more than staff executives' views of planning or was to be more than just another list of planning do's and don'ts. The requirements meant that the researcher had to spend a great deal of time at each research site.

To meet these requirements, case studies of three corporations—Dexter Corporation, General Electric Company, and Memorex Corporation—were done. The case studies of the Dexter Corporation and of the General Electric Company involved relationships that lasted approximately one year each. During this time, managers at multiple levels and from operating and staff units were interviewed. Key meetings were attended and key strategic issues or resource allocation decisions were investigated in detail. In addition, the chief executive officers of both companies were interviewed in depth.

The case study of the Memorex Corporation is based on trial transcripts from the *Memorex v. IBM* and *United States v. IBM* antitrust cases. While this is an unconventional source of administrative data, the richness of the data (Memorex's CEO testified a total of 10 days during the trials and all of his files were available for study) and the fact that much of the testimony dealt with Memorex's management practices suggested that it was an appropriate source for a case study. Moreover, trial transcripts have been used quite successfully by other business researchers.[18]

Following the development of the case studies, I formulated tentative answers to the research questions and developed a number of concepts to help understand what happened in the case studies. To elaborate these concepts and tentative answers, a third phase of the research consisting of several projects was conducted. First, six additional companies were studied in less detail than the original three, but with a focus on particular issues. Also a number of case studies written by other researchers were reviewed, and two data bases on the use of portfolio planning were analyzed. The first data base, collected and first analyzed by Philippe Haspeslagh, contains survey responses of over 300 firms

TABLE 1.1.   RESEARCH DESIGN

Phase	Research Undertaken
1	*Preliminary data collection* Interviews at six companies Interviews with twenty senior managers attending Harvard's Advanced Management Program
2	*Case research* Dexter Corporation General Electric Company Memorex Corporation Tentative conclusions formulated
3	*Elaboration of concepts and conclusions* Six additional companies studied Other case studies reviewed and analyzed Two data bases on use of portfolio planning analyzed Ten chief executives interviewed

on their use of portfolio planning.[19] The second, collected with Rod White, contains data on the relationship among corporate headquarters, business units, and portfolio planning.[20] Finally, interviews were conducted with 10 chief executive officers of *Fortune* 500 companies to explore the ways in which they had used and managed portfolio planning.

Through analysis of all of these sources of data collected in all three phases of the research and summarized in Table 1.1, I developed that the concepts and conclusions that make up this book.

PORTFOLIO PLANNING IN A BROADER PERSPECTIVE

As soon as we turn our attention from the content of portfolio planning techniques to their impact and actual uses, we must develop a broader perspective. If we are interested in how major decisions are made and how portfolio planning is used, it is not enough to focus solely on the slopes of experience curves, the growth rates of markets, and competitive cost structures. Other factors, such as who is going to prepare and review the strategic plans and what the CEO hopes to accomplish from the planning efforts, become relevant. While endless lists of additional consid- erations can be developed, the data collected in this research suggest that our perspective has to be broadened in two major ways if we are to assess both the impact and the use of portfolio planning techniques.

Evaluation of the impact of portfolio planning requires the perspective that strategic decisions are of several types. Given this perspective, it is likely that portfolio planning techniques will be very relevant and helpful for some strategic decisions and less so, or even misleading, for others. In Chapter 2, it is suggested that strategy has three levels: business strategy, corporate strategy, and institutional strategy. These levels, which roughly correspond respectively to the competitive strategies of business units, to decisions about which businesses to be in, and to the broader purposes of the enterprise, are related but different. Significantly, the impact of portfolio planning on these three levels of strategy has been different.

To assess how portfolio planning techniques are actually used requires a broad perspective of the forces that influence decision making. To maintain that strategic decisions are shaped solely by technical analyses is too narrow a view. Three other forces also shape these decisions: the agenda and style of the CEO, financial constraints, and administrative considerations. Each of these forces is described in Chapter 3, and here it is necessary only to recognize that, when portfolio planning techniques are used in major corporations, their use is in the context of organizational politics, financial realities, and chief executive preferences.

The Myths and Realities of Portfolio Planning

Through a broader perspective of what strategy is and what factors affect strategic decisions, portfolio planning techniques can be placed in the context of how they are actually used and modified to make strategy happen. This perspective, which emerged from analysis of the data collected in all three phases of the research, has helped to reveal a number of realities about portfolio planning that stand in contrast to the many myths that have developed.

These myths begin with the assertion that portfolio planning techniques are appropriate for all companies at all times.[21] In contrast, my research has led to the conclusion that the techniques are most frequently used for dealing with problems of corporate strategy as opposed to business or institutional strategy, and by companies whose financial resources are very limited. For other decisions and under other circumstances, companies make significantly less use, if any, of portfolio planning. Particularly in the case of business strategy decisions, choices made solely on the basis of an SBU's position on a portfolio matrix can be very inappropriate.

That the usefulness and applicability of portfolio planning are limited, however, does not justify another myth: that portfolio planning is a misguided effort and contributes to the lagging competitiveness of many American corporations.[22] The examples and data from this investigation suggest that, despite limitations, portfolio planning can help to improve the financial performance of ailing companies and can lead to such bold actions as the disposition of hopelessly weak businesses and the reallocation of the freed-up resources to high-potential businesses. Clearly the use of portfolio planning techniques can contribute to economic growth and reindustrialization rather than to economic decline.

Another myth is that portfolio planning is solely an analytic technique and its use need not affect how a company is organized and operates. On the contrary, my examples suggest that its use inevitably brings up a number of organizational and implementation issues. These include designation of the business units that will do planning, relationship of business units to the operating organization, determination of the level at which business unit strategies should be aggregated, decisions whether to label and publicize the strategic mandates of the business units, avoidance of the abandonment of mature businesses, and establishment of incentives and controls that avoid self-fulfilling prophecies. Far from being irrelevant, these issues of implementation are at the heart of what concerns top managers when they decide how, if at all, to use portfolio planning techniques.

The presence of these implementation issues reveals another sharp contrast between myth and reality. A common statement or implication is that there is one right way to use and implement portfolio planning. Yet because of the administrative problems that surround use of the techniques, companies are apt to modify the form of the techniques to avoid or mitigate some of the undesired consequences. Indeed the most striking thing about the companies studied in this research is that they have used portfolio planning for a variety of different purposes and have modified the techniques to best meet their objectives.

The most pervasive myth is that it takes a strong CEO to implement portfolio planning. The following comment, made by a senior partner of a well-respected consulting firm, typifies this point of view:

> Frankly, let me tell you that I am not interested in the administrative implications of our portfolio planning approach. The challenge is really analytical, not administrative. The way I see implementation is what I call the "rule of the Prince": Once the analysis is done, a strong CEO should see to it that the portfolio strategy gets implemented.[23]

It is true that portfolio planning requires the backing and involvement of the CEO. What is untrue is that the CEO has to be "strong and uncompromising" to see to it that planning gets implemented "like it's supposed to." The case studies of the most successful companies suggest that successful implementation of portfolio planning begins with a CEO who is clear about his or her own agenda and goals for the company and who understands the financial resources of the company, the administrative constraints to be faced, and the portfolio planning techniques themselves. It is then the job of the CEO to determine how to apply and modify portfolio planning to fit the needs of the company and to work in light of the other forces at play in the organization.

A CONCLUDING OBSERVATION

Since this research began, it has been hard not to notice the strong and changing attitudes toward portfolio planning techniques. At first, in the late 1970s, it was difficult to find anything but praise for portfolio planning. The culmination of this euphoria was a very positive, four-part series on strategic management that appeared in *Fortune* in October and November of 1981.[24] Only 13 months later, the same author wrote an article for the same magazine entitled "Corporate Strategists Under Fire," which criticized those very planning techniques that his previous articles had applauded:

> We're going to miss corporate strategy, that sweet collection of sure fire concepts—matrices, experience curves—that promised an easy win. Oh, it'll still be around here and there, showing its by now slightly grimy face in this corner or that, but things won't be as they were. Who can forget the excitement he felt when he first heard its siren song: **There are a few simple rules—understand them, make them your own, and you too can be a winner.**
>
> All that's over now. The strategy-consulting firms are pulling in their horns. Strategic planners within corporations are changing what they do—some are even losing their jobs.[25] [emphasis in the original]

These mood swings are not peculiar to the business press or to one particular magazine; managers and academics have also begun to reassess their previous enthusiasm. Perhaps portfolio planning has been just another managerial fad that will soon disappear.

The evidence from the companies studied in this investigation suggests otherwise. The theory of portfolio planning is simply too relevant to the problem of allocation of resources in diversified companies, and the approach can be used for too many different purposes, for it to disappear entirely. Instead it will remain an important strategic planning device in providing an overview of resource allocation choices and helping companies that face financial difficulties. Although it will be less important for companies in a strong financial position and for the resolution of issues of business and institutional strategy, it may still play a role as an aid in understanding their businesses and in identifying key issues.

A broader perspective of what strategy is and what forces influence its development and implementation, then, suggests that the techniques are not (and probably never were) remedies for all strategic problems, nor are they relevant for all companies. Their effective use begins with a CEO who knows his or her own objectives, who understands the company's administrative inheritance, and who appreciates the financial constraints and strategic issues facing the company. With this as a starting point, portfolio planning techniques can be modified to fit the CEO's agenda and the company's situation.

Portfolio planning techniques never were the cure-all that some claimed. But when properly used and modified, they can be an important tool for the chief executive in administering the processes of strategy formulation and implementation.

2
Strategy: Development and Implementation

In 1976, the Norton Company was reassessing the strategy of its Coated Abrasives Domestic business.[1] Beginning in 1971, the company had made extensive use of portfolio planning techniques with very positive results. Robert Cushman, President and CEO of Norton, commented:

> Our strategic planning has made a tremendous difference in the way the company is now managed. It gives us a much-needed handle to evaluate strategies for each of our many businesses.

The much-needed handles that Cushman referred to were the requirements that the strategic plans of each of Norton's 30 business units be reviewed in light of a PIMS (profit impact of marketing strategies) analysis of the business and that the appropriateness of the mission to build, maintain, or harvest the business be reviewed in light of portfolio analysis.

When these tests were applied to Norton's Coated Abrasives Domestic business, the results were at odds with what both division and corporate management were inclined to do with the business. For example, the PIMS analysis revealed that the low return on investment (ROI) of the business was at PAR. In other words, the business was performing as well as could be expected in light of industry conditions and its competitive position. The PIMS analysis concluded that the business should be managed to lose market share gradually to maximize its cash throw-off. Similarly, a growth-share matrix analysis of the business placed it well within the dog quadrant, with the implication that the business should be liquidated or divested.

What these portfolio techniques did not take into account was the Norton Company's commitment "to remain a worldwide leader in abrasives," which originated in Norton's long-standing presence and leadership in the abrasives field. Also overlooked was the judgment of the division manager that the business faced numerous operating problems (high wages and cost structure) that could be corrected. Since Norton's planning process emphasized the involvement and commitment of line managers, the opinion of the division manager was not taken lightly.

When the time came to make a decision, these latter factors concerning Norton's traditions prevailed. Rather than the business being harvested for cash as suggested by the planning analyses, investments were made to improve the division's cost structure and the business was given the strategic mandate to maintain market share. In discussing this decision, Norton executives indicated that, although the portfolio analyses were compelling, other strategic factors also had to be considered. Donald Melville, executive vice president, summarized this view when he explained that "we are not yet in a position where we can harvest a major segment of our abrasives business, because *that is the major guts of our company*" [emphasis added].

THREE LEVELS OF STRATEGY

The situation involving Norton's Coated Abrasives Domestic (CAD) business was a difficult one for top management because a number of different considerations, all strategic in nature, affected the decision. Not only did top management have to consider what approach would lead to the most success for the CAD business but also whether the company could afford the investment required and how CAD related to the overall concept of what the company was. It is the presence of multiple strategic considerations that not only makes the job of top managers, such as those at Norton, so difficult but that also leads to serious confusion about the definition of the word *strategy*.

The term *strategy*, or *corporate strategy*, is one of the most widely used and abused expressions in business today. As with most concepts that get popularized, its meaning has become more and more distorted as its popularity has grown. Today we can read about corporate strategy, marketing strategy, functional strategy, and strategic control. Unfortunately, the result often is confusion rather than insight. For example, one common area of confusion is the relationship between financial goals and strategy. While one can debate endlessly which should come first, in practice the two exist in a reciprocal relationship wherein strategy both shapes and is shaped by financial goals. For example, a financial goal to grow at a rapid rate will stimulate strategies to enter growth markets and either to exit mature industries or to build market share within these industries. On the other hand, commitment to a strategy of being a major player in a particular market will often result in financial goals that reflect conditions within that market.[2]

More germane to this research is the confusion caused by the numerous definitions of strategy. This is most unfortunate because, as we saw in the Norton example, often different sets of strategic considerations affect an issue. What is needed is a precise definition of strategy that can distinguish among the full range of strategic issues. Moreover, a precise definition is necessary to assess the impact of portfolio planning techniques on strategy and to understand situations such as the one at Norton, where portfolio planning affects some strategic issues but not others.

To arrive at a precise definition, it is useful to define three different levels of strategy that together form the overall strategy of the firm: *business strategy*, *corporate strategy*, and *institutional* strategy. Viewing strategy as having these three levels is consistent with Andrews' original concept of corporate strategy and reflects his most recent definition:

> Corporate strategy is the pattern of decisions in a company that determines and reveals its objectives, purposes, or goals, produces the principal policies and plans for achieving those goals, and defines the range of business the company is to pursue, the kind of economic and human organization it is or intends to be, and the nature of the economic and noneconomic contribution it intends to make to its shareholders, employees, customers, and communities. In an organization of any size or diversity, "corporate strategy" usually applies to the whole enterprise, while "business strategy," less comprehensive, defines the choice of product or service and market of the individual business within the firm.[3]

Recently other researchers, including Igor Ansoff and Hofer and Schendel, have begun to define strategy as consisting of multiple levels or aspects.[4] Unique in the identification of three levels of strategy are the notions of institutional strategy and of all three levels comprising the total strategy of the firm.

Business Strategy

Business strategy is commonly defined as "the determination of how a company will compete in a given business and position itself among its competitors."[5] Business strategy, then, refers to the competitive strategy of a particular business unit. A widely diversified company with numerous business units will have numerous business strategies.

It is important to note that business strategy refers to a specific description of how a business unit is to compete in its markets. Although the description includes the goals and mission of a business, it also contains the support policies that will be adopted to achieve those goals. A goal to dominate a market does not constitute a business strategy; statement of the goal must be augmented by a specific statement of what products, technologies, distribution channels, manufacturing techniques, and service policies will be employed to achieve the goal.

The strategy wheel is a useful device for illustrating the degree of specificity and consistency that must be achieved in a business strategy. As shown in Figure 2.1, business strategy has at its core the goals of the business and the concepts of how the business will compete. Of equal importance are precise definitions of key functional policies and that these policies be consistent with each other and with the objective of the business.

Figure 2.1.   The wheel of business strategy

Corporate Strategy

Corporate strategy is defined as the determination of the businesses in which a company will compete and the allocation of resources among the businesses. Corporate strategy decisions include divestitures, acquisitions, new business development projects, and the allocation of resources to each business. Obviously a single business company will not have a corporate strategy except in the sense that its corporate strategy is to compete in one business and that it will allocate all of its resources to that single business. For diversified companies, however, corporate strategy decisions are a key concern of top managers.

Institutional Strategy

Institutional strategy refers to the *basic character and vision of the company*. Though he did not label it as such, Andrews referred to institutional strategy in his definition when he stated that strategy determines "the kind of economic and human organization it is or intends to be, and the nature of the economic and noneconomic contribution it intends to make to its shareholders, employees, customers, and communities."[6]

IBM is an example of a company that has a particularly well-defined institutional strategy. The strategy began with the vision of Thomas Watson, Sr., that the company would become a major worldwide enterprise. This vision long preceded the advent of the computer and was described in a 1940 *Fortune* article:

> *"Ever onward," he told himself. "Aim high and think big figures; serve and sell; he who stops being better stops being good"* . . . *Mr. Watson caused the word THINK to be hung over the factory and offices.* . . . *Let him discourse on the manifest destiny of IBM, and you are ready to join the company for life.*[7]

IBM's institutional strategy has developed considerably since the days of Watson's exhortations. Today company publications stress three basic concepts that define the character of the company and serve to guide the organization's choices and behavior:

1. **Respect for the individual.** Respect for the dignity and the rights of each person in the organization.

2. **Customer service.** To give the best customer service of any company in the world.

3. **Excellence.** The conviction that an organization should pursue all tasks with the objective of accomplishing them in a superior way.[8]

As illustrated by IBM, a company's institutional strategy may pertain to its employees, to its customers, to its markets, or to how it competes. Some brief characterizations of each of these kinds of institutional strategy are listed in Table 2.1. In all of these examples, institutional strategy provides the *basic concepts and beliefs that guide the organization's choices and behavior.* And because institutional strategies embody what Donaldson and Lorsch[9] referred to as the company's belief system, organization members tend to identify and agree with the institutional strategy or leave the company. The comment of an employee of the Lincoln Electric Company is typical:

> It's like trying out for the high school football team. If you make it through the first few practices, you're usually going to stay through the whole season, especially after the games start.[10]

It is important to note, however, that institutional strategy is not the same thing as a corporate culture. In the sense that every organization has norms and accepted rules of behavior, all companies have a culture.[11] Yet all companies do not have institutional strategies, because the concept includes not only basic principles but also a vision of where the company is headed and how it will operate. Vision is what has directed IBM's total attention to the opportunities created by the advent of data processing; it is a specific concept of what a company is trying to become. Writing

TABLE 2.1.   CHARACTERIZATIONS OF
INSTITUTIONAL STRATEGIES

Pertaining to	Company	Institutional Strategy
Employees	Lincoln Electric	Guaranteed employment and wages for all workers in proportion to their productivity
	Delta	A family feeling
	Hewlett-Packard	Innovative people at all levels
Customers	Caterpillar	Spare parts availability within 24 hours around the world
	IBM	Customer service
	McDonald's	Fast service, consistent product, low price
Manner of Competing	Hewlett-Packard	High value, high margin, and innovation
	Texas Instruments	High volume, low margin, low costs
	McDonald's	High quality
	3M	Product innovation
Markets	Procter & Gamble	Packaged consumer products
	Dexter Corporation	Specialty industrial markets

in the *McKinsey Quarterly*, Fred Gluck has described the following characteristics of vision:

> . . . *the visions of the successful, excellent companies we have discussed were based not only on a clear notion of the markets in which they would compete, but also on specific concepts of how they would establish an economically attractive and sustainable role or position in that market. They were powerful visions grounded in deep understanding of industry and competitive dynamics, and company capabilities and potential. They were not mere wishful thinking as is the case with so many incomplete visions . . . the visions were generally directed at continually*

strengthening the company's economic or market positions or both in some substantial way.[12]

During the past two decades, the importance of institutional strategy has often been overlooked as attention has instead been focused on techniques of strategic analysis and issues of business and corporate strategy. Not surprisingly, in a paper delivered two years prior to publication of *In Search of Excellence*, Tom Peters[13] reported that in a survey he conducted of 65 companies, only 13 (20%) had a strong set of beliefs that guided their actions. But these 13 companies significantly outperformed the other companies in the sample.

Recently several very popular books have pointed to the importance of corporate culture, superordinate goals, corporate values, and corporate belief systems.[14] These books and concepts have served the important function of redirecting the attention of managers to these significant determinants of the success of their companies. But the concepts, which only describe existing norms and practices, do not by themselves constitute an institutional strategy unless they are combined with a vision of the company's future purposes and objectives. In his fascinating description of Schlumberger and its CEO Jean Riboud, Ken Auletta[15] has aptly described what we mean by institutional strategy. Auletta first described Schlumberger's strong norms of excellence and independent thought, and termed them "the Schlumberger Spirit." But he then added that CEO Riboud is concerned that the company will become complacent and therefore devotes his time to assuring that the Schlumberger Spirit is flexible enough to recognize and meet future challenges:

> One of Riboud's preoccupations is that Schlumberger will lose its drive as a company and grow complacent—a concern he had discussed on the plane to Houston. "Any business, any society has a built-in force to be conservative. The whole nature of human society is to be conservative. If you want to innovate, to change an enterprise or a society, it takes people willing to do what's not expected. The basic vision I have, and what I'm trying to do at

*Schlumberger, is no different from what I think should be done in
French or American society." In other words, sow doubt. Rotate
people. Don't measure just the profits in a given division—measure the man in charge, too, and his enthusiasm for change. . . .*

*Summing up, Riboud said, "If we lose the drive, and fear searching
for new technologies, or fear taking incredible gambles on new
managers," or fear to heed the voices of "other countries and
cultures, then we will become an establishment." If that happens,
Schlumberger may remain powerful and profitable for the mo-
ment, but ultimately it will decline. "It's easy to be the best,"
Riboud has said many times. "That's not enough. The goal is to
strive for perfection."[15]*

Institutional strategy, like business and corporate strategy, can
be managed and directed by strong corporate leadership. Just as
top management is considered responsible for the quality of business and corporate strategies, it is similarly accountable for institutional strategy.

Implications

The three levels of strategy just described have their roots in the
writings of many authors. They have been developed here to help
explain the impact portfolio planning systems have on strategy.
Simply put, the experiences of the companies studied suggested
that portfolio planning had had or was having a substantial impact on some strategic issues and a negligible effect on others. In
the Norton Company, for example, we saw that initially portfolio
planning had little impact on institutional strategy. And since
institutional strategy was one of the main determinants of the
objective to adopt for the Coated Abrasives Domestic business,
portfolio analyses played a minor role in the final decision. Of
course, Norton is just one company and one example. However,
with additional data, the concept of three levels of strategy should

enable us to state more precisely the level or levels of strategy on which portfolio planning has had its greatest impact.

STRATEGY DEVELOPMENT AND IMPLEMENTATION

The concept of three levels of strategy can help not only in assessing the impact of portfolio planning but also in understanding the processes of strategy formulation and implementation. This is especially significant in light of the importance of implementation and strategy development and the slow progress being made in understanding them. Indeed the academic literature on these topics has been bogged down in debates over whether formulation and implementation are separable and which of the processes precedes the other.[16]

One way to dismiss these arguments is simply to acknowledge that strategies are constantly being changed and revised. Once a strategy is developed, managers begin to implement it. But when problems or new opportunities are encountered, the strategy is often revised. Thus the processes of strategy development and implementation are both continuous and symbiotic.

While the research undertaken for this book has confirmed the interrelationship of strategy formulation and implementation, it has also pointed to differences in how the three levels of strategy are formulated and implemented and to important links between the processes. The notion that all three levels of strategy are being developed and implemented simultaneously and are constantly influencing each other is admittedly a complicated one. But a clear understanding of what these processes entail at each strategic level can enable us to move from academic questioning of whether implementation takes place (a phenomenon to which any executive will readily attest) to understanding of how the formulation and implementation of each level of strategy affect the other levels and are influenced by portfolio planning techniques.

Strategy Development*

Strategy development refers to the processes by which each of the three levels of strategy are formed. Henry Mintzberg has suggested that strategies are developed in one of three ways: they are conceived as the entrepreneurial insight of one individual, they develop in an ad hoc manner as a result of the organization reacting to current problems, or they develop as the result of systematic planning and analysis.[17]

While this list could be expanded or modified, the point is still the same—there are a variety of approaches to development of strategy. In addition, the process can involve different people or levels in the organization, ranging from the chief executive to division managers. As shown in Figure 2.2, the combination of *how* strategy is developed and *who* develops it provides a more complete description of the strategy development process. A statement that a company uses formal planning, for example, is not a

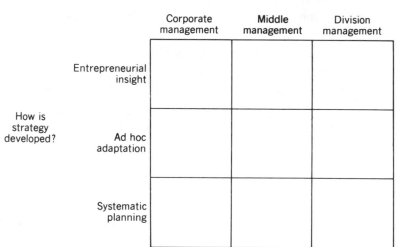

Figure 2.2.   Strategy development

*The terms *strategy development* and *strategy formulation* are used interchangeably.

complete description of how it sets strategy unless the statement also specifies who in the organization is involved in the planning effort. There is a great deal of difference between the CEO and his or her staff developing formal plans for a division and a division preparing the plan itself.

Finally it is important to recognize that, since there are three levels of strategy (institutional, corporate, and business), each must be developed and often the processes are different. Figure 2.3 illustrates how these three factors—how, who, and at what level—combine to describe the entire strategy development process. For example, in one company institutional strategy may be set by the CEO as a result of private insights, while business strategy is developed by planning teams in the divisions, and corporate strategy emerges as the result of decisions at all levels of the organization. Such a company would be guided by the CEO's sense of overall purpose and would produce well-developed busi-

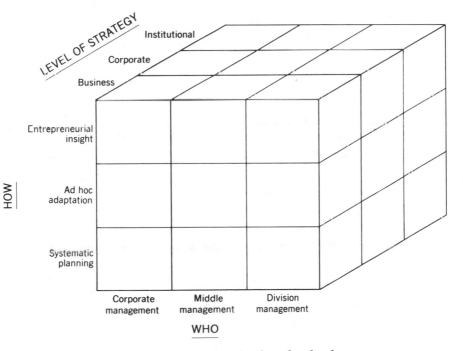

Figure 2.3. Development of the three levels of strategy

ness plans, but it would still be keeping its options open as to acquisition, divestiture, and resource allocation choices. In another organization both institutional and corporate strategy may be established at the corporate level as the result of detailed planning, while business strategy is developed in an ad hoc manner at the divisional level. This description probably is typical of those conglomerates that have thought in detail about acquisitions and divestitures, but have given less thought to the management of ongoing businesses.

That there are numerous ways to develop strategies is exemplified in the companies studied in this research. It points to the need for adjustment of the use of portfolio planning techniques to conform to the ways a company develops its strategies.

Strategy Implementation

Strategy implementation is the process of ensuring that strategy is embodied in all that an organization does.[18] The objective of implementation is to create fits between strategic objectives and the company's daily activities. For each level of strategy, there are important differences in the implementation task.

Implementation of business strategy requires the creation of *functional and administrative fits*. The creation of functional fits refers to the adoption and execution of policies in each of the functions—marketing, manufacturing, engineering, and finance—that reinforce the strategy. The following example illustrates how difficult this task can become:

> The manager in charge of a business that previously competed by producing unique products to order specifications, embarked on a new aggressive strategy. He believed he could increase the business's market share by selling the value of product availability rather than technology alone. The key to his approach was to release certain models to manufacturing before firm orders were in hand, thereby significantly shortening the delivery cycle.
>
> Months later, this manager began to have second thoughts about

this idea. For one thing, the models built in anticipation of demand required costly rework in order to match them to the orders ulti- mately received. Furthermore, customer complaints made it crys- tal clear that the publicized reduction in the delivery cycle had not been met. Missed schedules were also creating costly penalties.

An investigation proved the root of these problems to be the mea- surements used in district sales offices. For years, the bonuses of the sales engineers had been based on the dollar size of orders. Such a system prompted the engineers to give full rein to their customers' normal inclinations to demand tailored products rather than to worry about which model the customers ordered. Allusions to "king customer" were taken quite literally by field personnel. They did not recognize that their general manager's new strategy required a particular response from them.[19]

This example illustrates many of the problems general manag- ers encounter when trying to create the functional fits that are essential to the implementation of business strategy. Communi- cating strategy to the functional vice presidents (or even involving them in the strategy formulation process) is not always enough to ensure that functional policies reflect the strategy. This is because the basic character of the functions often leads to ingrained behav- iors that are not easily changed just because a general manager announces a new business strategy. Manufacturing's drive for standardization, marketing's for customer responsiveness, en- gineering's for innovation, and finance's for cost control are all very natural functional postures that extend deep into each func- tional area. Yet despite the difficulty of the task, these functional biases often must be overcome before a business strategy can be achieved.

The other task of implementation of business strategies is the creation of administrative fits that assure that the business's sys- tems and processes are consistent with and reinforce the strategy. These systems and processes include the organization structure, information systems, incentive and control systems, and decision processes. As with functional fits, the devising of each of these systems and processes so that it reflects business strategy is a difficult task requiring the involvement of the general manager, not just that of staff specialists.

Implementation of corporate strategy involves different tasks than does implementation of business strategy. To the extent that the corporate strategy concerns itself only with the acquisition and divestiture of businesses, implementation requires merely assembling the necessary staff resources to do the appropriate analyses and developing the contacts in the investment community to assure that acquisition candidates are brought to the attention of management.[20] When the corporate strategy also concerns itself with the relative allocation of capital to the divisions and with the greater growth of some businesses than others, the task of implementing corporate strategy is more complex. Here implementation requires creation of the appropriate organizational context—incentives, autonomy, level of responsibility—between the divisions and the corporate level so that each division will indeed pursue the objectives that the corporate level has in mind for it.

Implementation of institutional strategy is a process about which much less is known and that only recently has attracted the attention of researchers.[21] It involves the important tasks of choosing and educating (indoctrinating) employees as to the vision and values of the company and of managing the company over a long period in a way that is consistent with those beliefs and objectives. Indeed one of the distinguishing features of the companies cited in books such as *In Search of Excellence* and *Corporate Cultures* is the long time that they have adhered to their institutional strategies. Implementing institutional strategy seems to require consistency among many small actions and managerial practices over a long period. As Tom Peters has noted:

> Repeatedly and conspicuously, the chief executive officers of these companies exhibited a common pattern of behavior: namely, obsessive attention to a myriad of small ways of shifting the organization's attention to the desired new theme . . . consistency in support of the theme, usually over a period of years.[22]

Relationships Between Strategy Development and Implementation

In managing the development and implementation of the three levels of strategy, the CEO has to keep all three of the strategies consistent with the demands of the external environment and with each other. One view of how CEOs manage this process is the sequential one shown in Figure 2.4, wherein each level of strategy is first formulated and then implemented. Implicit in this view are the assumptions that strategy is set in a top-down manner and that formulation and implementation are discrete, independent activities.

While this sequential view is quite rational and is consistent with common prescriptions of how to use portfolio planning, it is not an accurate description of the strategic process.[23] In most companies, strategy is set and achieved as the result of a continuous process of adjustment between the formulation and implemention of each level of strategy. This interactive view of the strategic process is illustrated in Figure 2.5. Admittedly, this view is more complicated than the sequential one, but it does describe

Institutional strategy formulation

Institutional strategy implementation

Corporate strategy formulation

Corporate strategy implementation

Business strategy formulation

Business strategy implementation

Figure 2.4.   A Sequential view of the strategic process

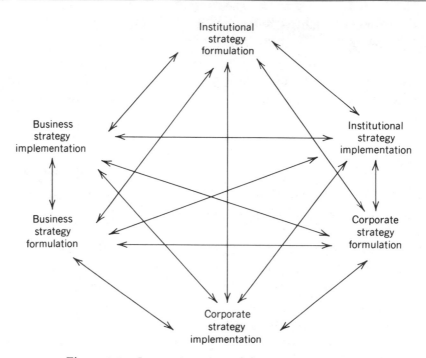

Figure 2.5. Interactive view of the strategic process

common strategic processes not accounted for in the sequential view. The first of these is bottom-up strategy development, wherein a strategy is conceived at a low level of the organization, is gradually implemented, and eventually affects the entire strategy of the firm. The interactive view is also consistent with the notion that strategies emerge over time, rather than being conceived at one point in time by "one big brain" at the top of the organization. This notion is similar to Quinn's conclusion after studying strategic change in nine companies:

> Dramatic new sets of strategic goals rarely emerge full blown from individual bottom-up proposals or from comprehensive corporate strategic planning. Instead, a series of individual, logical, and perhaps somewhat disruptive decisions interact to create a new structure and cohesion for the company. Top managers create a new consensus through a continuous, evolving incremental, and

often highly political process that has no precise beginning or end.[24]

The notion that the strategic process is interactive and continuous implies a need for top managers to adjust the way in which a technique such as portfolio planning is used. For as a tool of rational analysis, portfolio planning conceives of strategies as being set at the top of the organization and cascading downward in a series of market share and cash flow objectives for each business unit. For those companies that instead make these decisions in a continuous process of discussions among many levels of the organization, the ways in which portfolio planning is used need considerable modification.

CONCLUSION

In this chapter I have tried to clarify what is meant by business strategy, corporate strategy, and institutional strategy and how each of these strategies is developed and implemented and relates to the others. There were two reasons for this effort. First, the frequent use of the term *strategy* and the relative lack of research about strategy development and implementation implied the need to define and describe each of the terms as precisely and completely as possible. Second, in analyzing the impact and use of portfolio planning techniques in the companies studied, I found it necessary to develop these concepts and definitions in order to understand their impact and the variety and range of approaches in practice.

The Norton Company example illustrates this need. There is little question that portfolio planning has had a profound effect on this company and plays an important part in its decision processes. Yet in a decision as important as the market share objective and level of investment in the Coated Abrasives Domestic business, the conclusions of portfolio analysis were not followed. This situation can be understood by noting that as of 1976, portfolio planning had had an impact on Norton's business and corporate strategies but not on Norton's institutional strategy. The institutional strategy, which still valued leadership in the abrasives business, was a greater factor in determining the policies of the Coated Abrasives Domestic division than was portfolio analysis. In addition, the process by which Norton developed business strategies placed considerable emphasis on the recommendations of the managers running each business. That the managers running the Coated Abrasives Domestic business wanted to follow a strategy that contradicted the recommendations of portfolio analysis, and that they could offer persuasive evidence to support their position, constituted another important factor in the final decision.

Events such as those in the Norton Company are not unusual. The impact of portfolio planning on strategy is difficult to decipher without dividing strategy into its business, corporate, and institutional levels. And its impact on the formulation and implementation of each of these levels of strategy needs to take account of the fact that each of these processes is ongoing and affects the others.

3

The Forces Shaping Strategic Decision Making

In 1980, one of the companies I studied faced an interesting acquisition decision. This company, which was very serious about applying sophisticated strategic planning and resource allocation procedures, competed in five major business areas, each of which was headed by a group vice president. Of these five, the group in question competed in a very slowly growing industry and had been given the status of a cash cow with a strategic mandate to hold market share and to produce cash. The group vice president was one of the most senior and respected executives in the company and over the years had done an excellent job of running the group in accordance with its strategic mandate.

The group proposed in 1980 to make a major acquisition that would give it entry to a growing segment of its industry. The group and its management strongly supported the acquisition even though, at a cost of $30 million, it would not be cheap and would be inconsistent with their mandate to produce a high cash flow.

The CEO of the company, who had held the position for only a few months and was several years younger than the group vice president, had serious reservations about the acquisition. First, the expenditure contradicted the strategic mandate of the business to produce cash and only to maintain market share. Second, the investment left the group dependent on the same customers to whom its already slowly growing products were sold. On the other hand, the new CEO wanted to foster risk taking within the company and knew that the company as a whole could afford the acquisition.

When the time came to decide the issue, the CEO told the group vice president that he would prefer that the acquisition not be made. But if the group vice president were able to raise the funds from within his group, the CEO would not object.

Within days the group vice president was able to get the business units within his group to budget the necessary funds. Two months later the acquisition was consummated.

This example is typical of many that I observed during my research. It shows a major strategic decision being influenced by more than just portfolio analysis. This is not to denigrate the importance of portfolio planning or other analytic tools, such as industry and competitive analysis or scenario planning, which have clearly had a major impact on strategic decision making. In the company just described, for example, portfolio planning was one of the major forces that led to the divestiture of several weak businesses and to changes in the strategies of several others. Nonetheless, in making the acquisition decision, other factors, such as the seniority of the group vice president and the relatively new status of the CEO, and the CEO's interest in fostering risk taking, also influenced the decision.

While endless lists of factors that shape strategic decisions could be developed, the situations studied in this investigation repeatedly pointed to three forces in addition to portfolio and other forms of strategic analysis that played a role in shaping strategic decision making: administrative considerations, financial constraints, and the CEO's agenda and management approach (Figure 3.1). Interestingly, with the exception of the last factor, these forces correspond closely to what Donaldson and Lorsch's study of top management decision making in 12 companies called

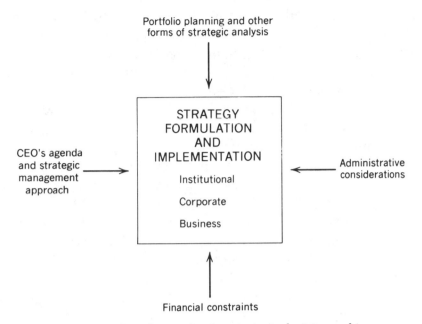

Figure 3.1.   Four forces shaping strategic decision making

the three primary constituencies whose expectations top managers must meet.[1]* The delineation in this study of the CEO as an additional major force in strategic decision making is not inconsistent with their findings, but it does place additional emphasis on the crucial role chief executives play in shaping strategy.

ADMINISTRATIVE CONSIDERATIONS

Portfolio planning and other forms of strategic analysis attempt to provide an objective assessment of a company's competitive strengths and weaknesses in the markets within which it operates.

---

*We refer to administrative considerations, financial constraints, and portfolio planning and other forms of strategic analysis. These correspond to what Donaldson and Lorsch termed the organizational constituency, the capital market constituency, and the product market constituency.

Such planning includes analyses of demand, industry structure, technological changes, raw materials supply, competition, and market segments. Portfolio planning techniques are a useful device for helping to make these assessments and are thus one of the forces that shape strategic decisions.*

As was illustrated by the acquisition decision, however, strategic decisions are also determined by administrative considerations. These considerations are reflected in organizational structures, systems, and processes and in the individual managers who not only make strategic choices but who also must translate these decisions into reality.

In a large diversified company, usually three sets of administrative considerations shape strategy. The first is the opinion of members of the company's *dominant coalition*. The dominant coalition refers to that limited number of employees who determine the organization's basic policies. The members of the dominant coalition, in addition to the CEO, may include other senior executives such as vice chairpersons or executive vice presidents, influential board members, large shareholders, and some experienced division managers. Although the membership of the dominant coalition will change over time, the opinions of this group are a major determinant of how strategies are formulated and implemented. For example, in the acquisition decision previously discussed, the fact that the group vice president was a senior executive with a long track record of excellent performance made his support of the acquisition a force with which the CEO had to reckon.

The second set of administrative considerations that affects strategic decision making is *the opinion and commitment of the*

---

*It is interesting to note that portfolio analysis and most other planning techniques have the common characteristic of focusing on the link between a company and its product market environment, while they typically overlook the relationship between the firm and labor and government. This is a nontrivial oversight in light of the significant effect government policy and labor relations can have on a company's results. While this limitation is important, it was not studied explicitly in this research.

top managers of affected divisions. For example, if the strategy of a division is being reappraised, the knowledge and opinions of the division managers will nearly always be solicited. Of course, the managers are not free to pursue any strategy they wish. But if they are not committed to or doubt the wisdom of a particular strategy, it is a rare chief executive who will not factor this consideration into the decision making. Sometimes this results in a slowdown in strategy formulation and implementation, while in other cases division managers are replaced. The important point is that the affected managers' level of commitment to a course of action is an important administrative consideration that shapes how and what major decisions are made.

Finally, strategic processes are shaped by *an organization's ability and capacity to implement a particular strategy.* An otherwise brilliant strategy that cannot be implemented or that would undermine morale is often not worth pursuing. Andrews has made the following observation to explain the important role of an organization's ability to implement strategy:

> Since faulty implementation can make a sound decision ineffective and effective implementation can make a debatable choice successful, it is as important to examine the processes of implementation as to weigh the advantage of available strategic alternatives.[2]

The significant impact that administrative considerations can have on the behavior of organizations has led some researchers to argue that large organizations cannot be purposefully directed and instead can only make incremental decisions that satisfy the needs of various organizational subgroups.[3] However, while administrative considerations can play a significant role in shaping strategic decisions, purposeful top managers can recognize and deal directly with political and administrative aspects of their organizations. In this regard, Bower has been most explicit:

> "Politics" is not pathology, it is a fact of large organization. Top management must manage its influence on "political" processes and then monitor the results of its performance.[4]

Finally, it is important to recognize that, while administrative considerations are one of the major forces shaping strategic choices, they are not the only ones. Indeed one of the major conclusions that Quinn drew from his study of strategic change in nine major companies was that both political and strategic factors influence change:

> All my data suggest that strategic decisions do not come solely from political power interplays. Nor do they lend themselves to aggregation in a single massive matrix where all factors can be treated quantitatively or even relatively simultaneously to arrive at a holistic optimum.[5]

FINANCIAL CONSTRAINTS

The way in which the top management of a company approaches strategic decisions is also affected by the company's financial constraints.* All companies face financial constraints in the sense that none has an endless supply of capital available to it. But companies do differ in the degree to which they are dependent on the external capital markets and in how much of a cushion exists between their need for funds and their internally generated sources of cash. The more these internal sources of funds exceed a company's need for capital, the less financially constrained the company is. Not surprisingly, most managements try to reduce their dependence on external capital markets and work to make their companies financially self-sustaining.[6]

When a company must rely heavily on external sources of capital, its overriding goal is to restore itself to a position of financial self-sufficiency, and this in turn can have a profound

---

*Not reaching financial goals can have the same effect on decision making as increasing financial constraints. In the companies studied here, however, the extent of financial constraints played a more significant role in shaping strategic decision making.

effect on strategic decision making. As Donaldson and Lorsch have noted, this is often reflected in a greater emphasis on return on investment:

> During times of heightened financial uncertainty or stress, these managers will also be particularly mindful of the rate of return on investment because of the importance accorded this figure by professional investors . . . . Therefore, the company's growth is secondary to its rate of return.[7]

It is important to note that most companies behave as if they were facing severe capital constraints long before there is even a threat of bankruptcy, once again because most companies attempt to finance their growth from internally generated capital, profits, and depreciation. New equity is rarely issued, and debt is issued only within the limits of maintaining a targeted capital structure.[8] When a company attempts to maintain a constant or slightly increasing dividend level and a stable capital structure, it is highly dependent on the profitability of current operations to fund its new investment. Consecutive decreases in either sales growth or profit margins will severely reduce the size of the capital budget and will necessitate difficult choices among investment projects that are competing for limited funds.

These points can be illustrated by projecting the income statement and the balance sheet of a hypothetical $500 million company. Table 3.1 shows the projected financial performance of such a company. The company is anticipating an annual sales growth of 15% and a 20% pretax return on sales for each of the next five years. The important numbers to note are the cash available for capital expenditures each year. These numbers total $104 million over the five-year period. What this means is that the division managers of this hypothetical company know that approximately $104 million is available for capital projects over the next five years.

Should sales growth or the return on sales decrease, the cash available for capital expenditures will fall dramatically. Figure 3.2 illustrates the implications of such declines. In Model 2, sales

TABLE 3.1.   PROJECTED PERFORMANCE WITH 15 PERCENT
SALES GROWTH AND 20 PERCENT PROFIT MARGIN
($ MILLION)

Item	Performance ($ Million)				
	Year 1	Year 2	Year 3	Year 4	Year 5
Sales	500	575	661	760	874
Pretax profits (before interest)	100	115	132	152	174
Net earnings	48	56	64	73	84
Dividends	19	22	26	29	34
Total assets	386	448	521	604	701
Current liabilities and debt	186	215	249	288	333
Equity	200	233	272	316	366
Cash Flow Analysis					
Net cash flow	51	58	67	77	88
Less: Expenditures for asset replacement	35	40	46	53	61
Cash available for capital expenditures	16	18	20	23	27
Cumulative cash available for capital expenditures	16	34	54	77	104

growth slows from 15% in the second year to 12% in the fifth year,
while pretax return on sales falls from 20% to 16%. In Model 3, the
declines are steeper, with sales growth slowing to 9% in year 5 and
pretax returns falling to 12%. In these models, however, *the company is still profitable and growing;* the only changes are *slower-
than-expected* sales growth and lower profit margins.

Given that this company attempts to maintain the same capital
structure and fairly stable dividends, the impact on the capital
budget is dramatic. As shown in Figure 3.2 by year 5 the cash
available for capital expenditures has fallen to $82 million in
Model 2 and to $59 million in Model 3. This decline in the capital
budget, from an expected $104 million to either $82 or $59 mil-
lion, would in turn put tremendous pressure on corporate man-

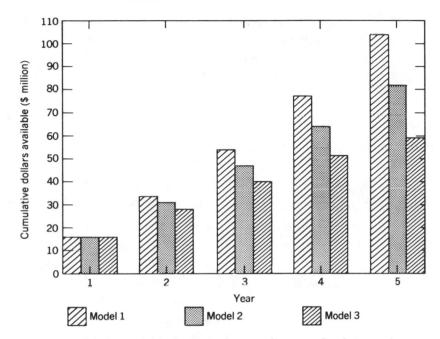

Figure 3.2. Funds available for capital expenditure under three performance scenarios. Model 1 has a constant growth rate and constant margins, Model 2 has a moderating growth rate and falling margins, while Model 3 has a falling growth rate and deteriorating margins.

agement to limit the allocation of scarce capital to divisions that are demanding more funds than the corporation can supply.

Companies that are financially constrained, then, face different strategic and resource allocation problems than companies that are not. The top management of capital-short companies is in need of tools, systems, and procedures that will help it in the unpleasant tasks of rationing capital and encouraging strategies of consolidation and focus. Companies in a strong financial position must still be vigilant in the allocation of resources, but the problem facing their top managers is more one of encouraging their divisions to propose enough high-return projects and to pursue broad enough strategic objectives.

These very different postures and needs do have an important effect on strategic decision making. For example, in the acquisi-

tion decision described earlier, the fact that the company had
been producing cash surpluses in recent years and was in a very
strong financial position had a very positive effect on the decision
to approve the $30 million expenditure. Had the opposite been
true, a much different decision might have been made.

THE CEO's AGENDA AND MANAGEMENT APPROACH

The last force that repeatedly plays a major role in the shaping of
strategic decisions is the CEO. Simply put, business organizations
do respond to the desires (and even the whims) of their chief
executive. To understand how strategic decisions are made or
how a tool such as portfolio planning is used, the goals and
management approach of the CEO must be closely examined.

The CEO's Agenda

There is no dearth of theory about what the job of the CEO entails.
There is also little consensus. For example, a large body of literature attests to the overwhelming impact of the CEO on corporate
affairs and to the importance of appointing to the job someone
with broad vision and leadership skills.[9] According to this view,
CEOs are in the center of decision making and have clear ideas
about what business, corporate, and institutional strategies they
want to achieve. Others, however, point to the limited power of
CEOs and to the diversity of large companies, which make it
virtually impossible for the CEO to understand all of the businesses and markets in which the firm competes.[10] According to
this view, the CEO cannot possibly formulate strategies, and this
task is dispersed throughout the organization.

Both of these views can be reconciled, however, by recognizing
that most chief executives pick a few issues on which they focus
their attention. As described by Wrapp:

> *The second skill of the good manager is that he knows how to save*
> *his energy and hours for those few particular issues, decisions, or*

> problems to which he should give his personal attention . . . .
> Recognizing that he can bring his special talents to bear on only a
> limited number of matters, he chooses those issues which he be-
> lieves will have the greatest long-term impact on the company, and
> on which his special abilities can be most productive. Under ordi-
> nary circumstances he will limit himself to three or four major
> objectives during any single period of sustained activity.[11]

In other words, for three or four major issues, CEOs do become
deeply involved in the outcome of strategic decisions. For other
strategic questions, however, the substantive involvement of the
CEO is much more limited.

These few issues on which the CEO focuses his attention are
what John Kotter calls the general manager's agenda. Kotter also
found that CEOs tended to get deeply involved only with issues
that were on their agenda:

> The GMs [general managers] . . . did not waste time and energy
> intervening where it wasn't really necessary; they gave people who
> were capable of doing a good job the authority to do just that. They
> actively involved themselves in execution only when they felt
> something on their agenda would not be accomplished without
> their aid.[12]

Management Approach

In addition to choosing an agenda, a CEO must determine the way
in which he or she will attempt to affect the processes of strategy
formulation and implementation. Although there are countless
ways that CEOs approach this task, a few of the major dimensions
that distinguish various approaches can be identified.

One of these dimensions is whether the CEO chooses to manage
the outcome of a strategic decision or to manage the process by
which the decision is made. In the former case, the CEO knows the
desired outcome and becomes directly involved to ensure that the
outcome is both adopted and achieved. In the latter case, the CEO
is less concerned with the outcome per se and instead aims to
ensure a thorough review of all options and that all affected
parties are consulted.

Another difference in the way CEOs affect decision making is the extent to which they *pay attention to administrative constraints*. As noted earlier, these administrative constraints refer to the extent of agreement among the members of top management and the willingness and capability of subordinates to implement a strategy. In some instances, CEOs are reluctant to adopt or implement decisions that are not fully supported within their organization, while in others, they are willing to confront these obstacles.

The specific management approach that a CEO takes depends on many factors, not the least important of which is his personal management style. Here, however, we can note that the approach also depends on whether the issue is on the chief executive's agenda. For issues that are high on the agenda, a CEO is more likely to manage outcomes and to not be dissuaded by administrative constraints.

It has also been observed that CEOs tend to adopt different management approaches depending on the stage of their tenure. For example, early in their careers, CEOs are more concerned with establishing interpersonal relationships and their expectations with key subordinates than with managing major issues.[13] This usually means that they manage processes and pay considerable attention to administrative constraints. For example, Kelly has reported that:

> New CEOs do not attack the large strategic issues as the first priority. They look to the structure of relationships and responsibilities —both formal and informal—in the organization as the first area for thought, concern, and change. They seek to change the infrastructure to gain control of the organization, and then they consider strategy.[14]

After key relationships have been established and major responsibilities have been divided and assigned, CEOs do formulate their agenda. At this point, CEOs are likely to manage aggressively those issues that are highest on their agenda.[15]

In the later years of a CEO's tenure, his or her attention will increasingly shift to the selection of a successor. As this occurs, strategic decisions tend to take on less significance than the task of structuring relationships and responsibilities so that key contenders can be equitably evaluated and compared.

CONCLUSION

In this chapter we have reviewed the three forces that, in addition to portfolio planning and other forms of strategic analysis, repeatedly play a major role in shaping strategic decisions. These forces, which are diagrammed in Figure 3.1, help to explain why the conclusions of portfolio analysis sometimes are not followed, even by the most ardent supporters of the technique. For example, in the acquisition decision presented, the fact that the company had ample financial resources, that group-level management strongly supported the proposal, and that the CEO was still new in his job and was developing relationships with key subordinates all pointed toward approval of the acquisition, even though a portfolio analysis concluded the group should not be the recipient of large cash investments.

Perhaps more important, identification of the forces also suggests the need for chief executives to modify and shape the use of portfolio planning to be consistent with their own objectives and management approach, their company's financial resources, and administrative realities. Sometimes this consistency between the forces exists naturally and portfolio theory can be readily applied to help the CEO achieve his objectives. But when the other forces suggest a different direction than does portfolio planning, chief executives can and, as we shall see, do modify the use of the techniques.

Part 2

The Practice of
Portfolio Planning

4

The Uses of Portfolio Planning

The theory of portfolio planning provides a way of allocating resources to divisions that is consistent with their business potential. As described in Chapter 1, this contribution of portfolio planning helps to overcome some of the most serious limitations of traditional capital budgeting procedures and helps to explain the appeal of portfolio planning techniques to senior managers. In my study of the experiences of companies, however, it became apparent that portfolio planning techniques were being used for purposes other than simply resource allocation. In other words, chief executives have found and created ways in which portfolio planning can help them with their job. Specifically, portfolio planning is commonly used in three related yet very different ways: to facilitate the allocation of resources, to improve the quality of strategic thinking at the business unit level, and to increase corporate management's understanding of the business units and of the overall corporate portfolio.

These uses of portfolio planning are significant for several reasons. First, they illustrate the ability of managers to adapt a theoretical tool to a variety of purposes—another explanation of portfolio planning's widespread use, since each additional use of portfolio planning expands the number of companies that may find it beneficial. This ability of managers to use portfolio planning for several purposes shows that the theoretical description of portfolio planning should not necessarily be equated with the way the tool is actually used in practice, and it underscores the important role chief executives play in determining how and why the techniques are used. Equally important, the fact that portfolio planning can serve different purposes helps to explain the wide variety of approaches companies have taken in managing the numerous administrative issues that arise when the techniques are put into practice. These issues and approaches are discussed in the next two chapters. In this chapter, the different uses of portfolio planning are described and illustrated.

RESOURCE ALLOCATION

Because the theory of portfolio planning provides a way for companies to link investment decisions and business planning, it is not surprising that they have used the techniques to facilitate resource allocation. A closer examination of this use, however, suggests that it can serve two quite different resource allocation purposes. The first is promotion of divestitures and corporate restructuring; the second is guidance of capital allocations within the company.

Divestitures and Corporate Restructuring

The Mead Corporation is a good example of a company that used portfolio planning to facilitate divestiture decisions and corporate restructuring.[1] During the conglomerate era of the 1960s, Mead, an integrated paper manufacturer, diversified into numerous unrelated areas. By the early 1970s, it had acquired over 40 companies in such wide-ranging industries as castings, coal, rubber products, and consumer education. Despite this diversification, Mead's financial performance declined, with 1970 marking the low point. Return on net assets was only 3.7% and return on equity was even lower—2.9%.

To help correct this situation, Mead began to apply vigorously the techniques of portfolio planning. In particular, all of Mead's businesses were classified and arrayed on a growth-share matrix. James McSwiney, Chief Executive Officer, described the results of this analysis:

> In 1972, when we classified our businesses on this matrix, we found many were competing in low growth segments with low market share. We decided that by 1977 we should eliminate those low growth and low market share businesses. . . . Our first step was to dispose of 15 businesses where it was not practical to become a leader.

> They were essentially the low growth, low market share businesses. This step generated $80 million in cash, plus it saved $25 million we would have had to invest if we'd kept them. Especially important, these actions immediately improved our mix of businesses and the total return from our assets.[2]

As illustrated by this example from the Mead Corporation, portfolio planning is particularly well suited to promoting divestitures. One reason for this is that the techniques identify a group of businesses that are the most likely sale candidates. Equally important, portfolio analysis enables top managers to make divestiture decisions in a detached and analytic manner. This detachment can be a useful antidote to the emotional appeals of the affected divisions that nearly always accompany divestiture decisions.[3]

Portfolio planning is frequently used for divestiture decisions because divesting weak businesses can have such a dramatic effect on cash flow and return on investment. As we saw at Mead, divestitures generated $80 million in cash, and by 1977 return on net assets had increased nearly threefold, to 10.4%. Much of this increase in return on net assets was attributable to the sale of Mead's least profitable businesses.

Table 4.1 illustrates how the use of portfolio planning to promote divestiture can have a dramatic effect on the ROI (return on investment) of a hypothetical company. In this example, the company's ROI is 10%, but this figure is merely the *average* of what all of the company's divisions are earning. As shown in the table, divisional ROIs range from a high of 25% to a low of minus 2%. Portfolio planning techniques will highlight the low returns and presumably weak competitive positions of divisions H, I, and J. If management divests those divisions, total company ROI rises dramatically. As shown in the table, divestment of divisions H and I would result in a rise in the ROI of the total company from 10% to 12.75%. If division J were also sold, ROI would increase to over 14%.

What to do with the cash brought in from the sale of divisions is the next issue facing managers who embark on programs of divestiture. An obvious approach is to invest the funds in the company's remaining businesses. But another common approach is to

TABLE 4.1. IMPACT OF PORTFOLIO PLANNING AND DIVESTITURES ON A COMPANY WITH 10% AVERAGE RETURN ON INVESTMENT (ROI)

Before Portfolio Planning		After Portfolio Planning	
Division	ROI%	Action No. 1	Action No. 2
A	25%	No change	No change
B	23	No change	No change
C	17	No change	No change
D	11	No change	No change
E	10	No change	No change
F	8	No change	No change
G	5	No change	No change
H	3	Divest	Divest
I	0	Divest	Divest
J	−2	No change	Divest
Total company[a]	10	12.75% ROI	14.14% ROI

[a]Assumes all divisions are of equal size.

use the cash to acquire businesses in new areas of greater opportunity, commonly referred to as *corporate restructuring.*

An example of a company that has used portfolio planning to facilitate restructuring is the Monsanto Company. Monsanto began using portfolio planning in the mid 1970s, following several years of lackluster performance. What portfolio planning revealed was the weakness of Monsanto's very large commodity chemicals business and a lack of growth businesses within the company. As a result, in recent years Monsanto has disposed of over $1 billion worth of assets that were formerly employed in its commodity chemicals businesses. Those assets have been redeployed in two major growth areas, health care-biotechnology and highly engineered and manufactured products, by means of acquisitions, venture capital funding, joint ventures, and research and development. While Monsanto's restructuring is by no means complete, it is clear that portfolio planning has been used to create a company that is much different from the one that until recently had over 90% of its assets in basic chemical businesses. Richard Mahoney, Monsanto's CEO and an enthusiastic proponent of portfolio planning, predicts where the restructuring is heading when he explains that "you're going to see a Monsanto in the Nineties that's about one-third a biological company . . . one-third a chemical company . . . and one-third a mechanical goods company. . . . Now that's quite a difference."[4]

Despite the excitement generated by bold restructurings such as Monsanto's, it is important to acknowledge that this strategy does not guarantee success. The ability of managers to predict profitable growth opportunities is limited, and the high prices paid for acquisitions in growth fields often preclude the acquiring company's earning a reasonable return on its investment.[5] At Monsanto, for example, return on equity in 1982 was only 9.5%, lower than it was when the restructuring began.

A dramatic example of some of the pitfalls of corporate restructuring is given by Bendix Corporation. What is missing in most of the popular accounts of this story is the fact that Bendix's ill-fated attempt to acquire Martin Marietta was part of a corporate restructuring effort in which Bendix had disposed of its forest products business and its interest in the metals business and was seeking to redeploy the cash from those divestitures in a high-technology electronics business. William Agee, CEO, explained these actions in the 1980 and 1981 annual reports:

> These major strategic actions [divestitures] converted approximately $500 million in lower-return assets into a liquid portfolio. . . . Our future, we firmly believe, lies in a reemphasis on technology.[6]

While Bendix's failure to acquire Martin Marietta and its own takeover by Allied Corporation had several causes, Bendix's own program of corporate restructuring was at least partially responsible for the disastrous outcome. It was this program that put Bendix in the market to acquire a large technology-driven company. Yet as the results show, it was easier for Bendix to articulate this strategy than to achieve it.

Capital Allocations Within the Company

Divestitures and corporate restructuring focus the attention of company management outside the corporation in a search for buyers and sellers of businesses. However, portfolio planning is also frequently used to guide resource allocation decisions within companies.

General Electric is probably the company most frequently cited as having used portfolio planning for this purpose.* Of course, GE has made some divestitures and acquisitions. But with the exception of the sale of its computer business (which preceded the introduction of portfolio planning by more than a year) and of the purchase and subsequent disposition of Utah International, which were high-level CEO decisions, GE's divestitures and acquisitions have been of minor significance compared with the shifts in resource allocation within the company. Reginald Jones, GE's

---

*See Chapter 10 for more information on the General Electric Company.

CEO from 1973 to 1981, explained in the 1973 annual report how GE would use portfolio planning for internal resource allocation:

> *Another source of confidence for us is the continued development of a strategic planning system that provides a strong discipline for differentiating the allocation of resources—that is, investing most heavily in areas of business that we identify as offering the greatest leverage for earnings growth, while minimizing our investments in sectors we see as growing more slowly or remaining static.*[7]

Three years later, in the 1976 annual report, Jones explained the results of these efforts:

> *Comparing the company today with the General Electric of only a few years ago shows that, in selectively allocating our resources to the growth opportunities identified through strategic planning, we have developed decidedly different sources of earnings and a different mix of businesses, whose potentials for profitable growth exceed those of our historic product lines.*[8]

Beginning in the early 1970s, then, General Electric's top management consciously chose to use the cash from the company's traditional power systems and industrial businesses to fuel growth in the engineered materials, financial services, information services, and medical systems businesses. Significantly, GE did not divest its traditional businesses, but sought only to allocate fewer resources to these more mature businesses. Also GE's growth did not come from acquisitions but from the internal development and allocation of resources to new businesses. Two prominent examples are GE's engineered materials business, which was started in the 1960s and whose sales were almost $2 billion by 1980, and computed tomographic (CT) scanners, a new market in which GE's share was over 70%. Table 4.2 summarizes the dramatic shift in the sources of General Electric's profits that resulted from the differentiated allocation of resources.

Jack Welch, GE's CEO since April 1981, has expressed a similar intention to assure that General Electric allocates resources to its growth businesses:

TABLE 4.2.   GENERAL ELECTRIC'S BUSINESS MIX

	Percent of Total Profits	
	1968	1979
Electrical equipment	80	47
Materials	6	27
Services	10	16
Transportation	4	10
International business	16	40

I won't put a lot of money into some old smokestack industries. We have somewhere between 60 to 75 percent of our company positioned in a high-growth mode. My intention is to assure that we put our resources behind these businesses. We shouldn't invest because we hope a business will get better and our investments aren't venture capital. I call it building from strength.

BUSINESS UNIT PLANNING

Whether it be to facilitate divestitures and corporate restructuring or to facilitate internal resource allocations, use of portfolio planning for the purpose of allocating resources places decision making in the hands of top management. As was noted in our discussion of strategy development, however, strategies can also be developed at other levels of the organization. And indeed, many companies use portfolio planning not to allocate resources from the top of the company but to improve the quality of the business strategies that the business units develop for themselves. This constitutes the second major use of portfolio planning: to improve the quality of strategic thinking at the divisional or business unit level.

The need for sound strategic thinking at the business unit level is one that all large diversified companies face, because corporate managers have neither the time nor the knowledge necessary to develop strategies for such a wide range of businesses. As a result, this task is typically left in the hands of strategic business unit (SBU) managers, with corporate management involved in establishing the format of the plans and in reviewing and approving them. What many companies have found is that requiring their SBUs to do portfolio planning can help to improve the quality of their business unit strategies.

Donald Melville, CEO of the Norton Company, explained why he uses portfolio planning for this purpose:

> We use portfolio planning to help us manage our businesses. This is not to say that we won't get rid of some businesses. But overall, we are committed to the industries that we are in and want to take steps that will help us to be successful in them over the long term.
>
> The result of using portfolio planning this way has been that our line organization has learned to think strategically. This takes time to accomplish, but once you have achieved it, it gives you a tremendous advantage in the marketplace.

The Dexter Corporation is one company that has used portfolio planning almost exclusively to improve the quality of business unit plans.* In fact, Dexter's corporate managers do not differentiate the allocation of resources to its divisions. Instead each division is managed as a "tub on its own bottom" and is responsible for managing the several strategic business segments within the division in a way that balances the division's sources and uses of cash. This practice stands in sharp contrast to the theory underlying portfolio planning, but it is consistent with Dexter's use of portfolio planning not to facilitate top-down resource allocation decisions but to improve the quality of business plans. At Dexter, for example, each business segment is required to undertake and explain the results of extensive PIMS (profit impact of marketing strategies) analyses of their business as a requirement of the planning process. In this way, portfolio planning becomes an input to a division's or business unit's thinking about its strategy.

Worth Loomis, Dexter's president, explained this use of portfolio planning in considerable detail:

*See Chapter 9 for more information on the Dexter Corporation.

Portfolio planning tools, such as PIMS and the growth-share matrix, confront division management with information that forces them to think strategically. Without this information, division managers tend to think only about their own business. The portfolio tools force them to think about their business in relation to the marketplace and in relation to the other opportunities the company has.

The important thing about our planning forms, such as the PIMS input forms, is that they force our divisions to confront certain information and the conclusions of certain analyses. I guess I still believe strongly in decentralization and that decisions and insights about how to compete should come from those people closest to the marketplace. It continues to impress me, but I have repeatedly found that if you put the right information in front of people, the right decisions will emerge.

Portfolio planning shouldn't be used, in my view, to allocate resources, but as an information tool to help everyone think about strategy and resource allocation decisions. Another reason why I feel this way is that I'm really not that much of a believer in great plans or in hitting home runs in business. The notion that you can allocate resources or restructure corporations from the top is a "home run" mentality and I have always tried to avoid that mentality. Instead, I try to work very hard to get all of our businesses to do things a little bit better each year. If you can do this over time, you usually end up earning superior returns and beating your competitors as they make mistakes.

Loomis' comment and the experiences of Norton and other companies suggest that use of portfolio planning can help to improve the quality of business plans in several ways. First, it helps to ensure that business strategies come to terms with the unit's market share or competitive position and with the growth or general attractiveness of the industry, and that specific goals are set in these areas. In this way, portfolio planning can help to overcome the lack of specificity that characterizes many strategic planning efforts. Furthermore, when business units are asked to reconcile their strategies with extensive outside analyses of their businesses, such as occurs at both Dexter and Norton with the PIMS reports, the result can be a marked increase in the quality of strategic thinking at the business unit level.

CORPORATE MANAGEMENT UNDERSTANDING

The third typical use of portfolio planning is for gaining understanding of individual business units and the company's overall portfolio of businesses. Again this use of portfolio planning is not predicted by the theory; it is a consequence of the diversity of most large companies, which hinder corporate managers from attaining full understanding of their businesses. By focusing the attention of senior managers on just a few variables, portfolio planning provides a way to understand individual businesses and the composition of the overall portfolio of businesses.

This use of portfolio planning is particularly prevalent early in a CEO's tenure, when the CEO needs to gain at least a rudimentary understanding of the numerous businesses within the company. For example, shortly after Jack Welch became CEO of General Electric in early 1981, he asked for all of GE's businesses to be arrayed on a growth-share matrix so he could determine what percentage of GE's businesses were in growth markets and occupied the number 1 or 2 position in their market. This analysis was much less sophisticated than what GE's corporate planners had been doing, but it provided Welch with a useful overview of the positioning of GE's businesses.

Another example of a new CEO using portfolio planning to gain an understanding of the company's businesses is Edward Hennessy's early experiences at Allied Corporation.[9] One of Hennessy's first actions was to begin a portfolio planning process that would provide him with basic data on each of Allied's businesses and an overview of Allied's portfolio. This analysis revealed that Allied was too dependent on its oil and gas business for future growth and that, excluding this business, 75% of Allied's businesses competed in mature industries. As a result of this analysis, Hennessy was able to articulate more specific strategies, such as the need to reposition Allied's mature businesses and to acquire a major business in a growth market.

Although the use of portfolio planning to increase understanding of businesses usually occurs early in a CEO's tenure, some CEOs use it for this purpose throughout their tenure. Robert

Cushman, chief executive officer of the Norton Company from 1971 to 1980, explained his reason for doing this:

> We continued to use portfolio management as a way to develop an understanding of our businesses. The major change from the early years was that early on we used it to understand our individual businesses and what we needed to do within each of them. Over time our focus shifted more to looking at the distribution of our businesses and the composition of our overall portfolio. It was this sort of analysis that directed us in the mid-1970s to look for a third leg of our company and that in the late 1970s led us to begin looking for a fourth leg, a task that we still have not accomplished.
>
> So over time, to me, the real value was the constant thinking it stimulated about our corporate portfolio and in providing a way for me to ask whether we were in the businesses that we should be in. I find it very easy to think in terms of pictures and continued to find portfolio screens to be a great benefit in thinking about these problems.

James Ferguson, CEO of General Foods, gave a similar explanation:

> In our recent strategic changes, portfolio planning techniques and categories were not used. However, in terms of helping us to think about our overall business, to understand it, and to generate the agenda of what we had to do, portfolio planning was very useful. But it was useful as a way of understanding and thinking, rather than as a way of managing and categorizing businesses.

An analogy can be made between use of portfolio planning to increase corporate management's understanding of the business units and the overall corporate portfolio, and the arrangement of the cards and counting the points in a bridge hand. Both activities can be very helpful in providing a basic, albeit incomplete, understanding of a situation. Even when more sophisticated techniques are used, the knowledge of how many points a bridge hand has or the basic configuration of the corporate portfolio can still be extremely useful.

This use of portfolio planning, to increase top management's understanding, is seldom noted but may well be its most frequent application. By focusing attention on just a few variables, such as market growth and market share, portfolio planning provides top managers with a way to gain a rudimentary understanding of their businesses and of the composition of their overall portfolio. After gaining this basic understanding, most corporate managers seek more detailed understanding of their company and pursue a variety of strategies. For example, Jack Welch has been pursuing growth and business development in General Electric, while Ed Hennessy has sought to reduce Allied's reliance on oil revenues. But even as these directions are pursued, the tools of portfolio planning can and are used to provide the basic understanding and rationale of more detailed strategies.

RELATING THE THREE USES

The three uses of portfolio planning that have been identified are distinct in the sense that they serve very different purposes and that some companies concentrate on only one of them. It is important to note, however, that often portfolio planning is used in more than one way and that its use at all leaves open the possibility that it will be applied for any of the three purposes. This is particularly true over time, as use shifts in response to changing company priorities. For example, the use of portfolio planning to improve corporate understanding of the businesses is often followed by use of the techniques to restructure the company or to upgrade business unit planning. Both General Electric and Allied are good examples of this phenomenon.

Further evidence of the presence of all three uses of portfolio planning comes from the survey Philippe Haspeslagh conducted of 345 *Fortune* 1000 companies. As shown in Table 4.3, in response to a question on the impact of portfolio planning, the managers in these companies indicated that portfolio planning had led to a sizable improvement in the quality of business strategic plans, corporate management's understanding of the individ-

TABLE 4.3.   IMPACT OF PORTFOLIO PLANNING: RESULTS OF SURVEY OF 345 *FORTUNE* 1000 COMPANIES

Impact of Portfolio Planning with Respect to:	Continuum				
	Negative Impact	No Impact	Sizable Improvement	Dramatic Improvement	
	0	1	2	3	4	5
The quality of business strategic plans				X* (2.88)		
Corporate management's understanding of individual businesses				X (3.22)		
Corporate management's ability to allocate resources across businesses			X (2.98)			

*X = average of all responses.

Source of data: Philippe C. Haspeslagh, "Portfolio Planning Approaches and the Strategic Management Process in Diversified Industrial Companies" (DBA Dissertation, Harvard University Graduate School of Business Administration, 1983).

ual businesses, and corporate management's ability to allocate resources across businesses. While the presence of all three uses of portfolio planning is the most striking feature of the response, also noteworthy is that, of the three uses, the improvement of corporate management's understanding of individual businesses received the highest average rating. This result is consistent with other data Haspeslagh collected, which indicated that, whereas

75% of his sample used portfolio planning techniques at the corporate level, only about 50% used them throughout their company.[10] These data, as well as the case and interview data collected in this research, suggest that portfolio planning's greatest usefulness may well be in providing a way for top management to understand the many businesses within the corporation rather than in facilitating resource allocation, as its underlying theory suggests.

As shown in Table 4.4, the uses of portfolio planning can also be related to the level of strategy that is most affected by each use and to the CEO management approach and process of business strategy development that are most consistent with each use. For example, use of portfolio planning to allocate resources has its greatest impact on corporate strategy and is most consistent with a CEO who is trying to achieve specific resource allocation outcomes, and with a business strategy development process that is heavily influenced by corporate management directives. In contrast, use of portfolio planning to improve business unit planning places the emphasis on business strategy and is more consistent with CEOs who prefer a process of strategy development that is heavily influenced by lower-level suggestions. One very important conclusion suggested by the analysis summarized in Table 4.4 is that none of the uses of portfolio planning affects a company's institutional strategy. Indeed this conclusion is corroborated by the case and interview data, as discussed in detail in Chapter 7.

Other Uses

The three uses of portfolio planning have been identified from an analysis of the companies studied and from the interviews undertaken during this research. They describe the major managerial objectives or uses that portfolio planning has served. Portfolio planning does have other applications, however, but most of these are for analytic rather than managerial purposes. For example, analysis of the business portfolios of competitors can be ex-

TABLE 4.4. RELATING THE USES OF PORTFOLIO PLANNING

Use	Level of Strategy Affected	CEO Management Approach	Process of Business Strategy Development
Resource allocation Restructuring	Corporate	Manage outcomes	Heavily influenced by corporate level
Internal allocations	Corporate	Manage outcomes	
Business unit planning	Business	Manage process	Developed by business unit management
Corporate management understanding	Business or corporate	Manage outcomes or manage process	Unclear

tremely valuable in strategic planning, in that it can suggest how likely competitors are to invest in certain of their businesses. This application of portfolio planning techniques and many others, however, are essentially technical.

One additional use of portfolio planning that managers frequently mention is its facilitation of communication about strategy because of its language system. While there is little question that the succinct language, terms, and concepts of portfolio planning do facilitate communication, this is a by-product of use of the approach and is seldom the *reason* companies use such planning. The companies and managers studied here have used portfolio planning for one of the three purposes described, and over time the continued use of the approach has facilitated and improved communication about strategy. This improved communication should not be regarded as a principal purpose of portfolio planning but rather as a very positive by-product of the successful implementation and continued use of the approach.

CONCLUSION

The widespread adoption of portfolio planning and its enduring use within companies would be difficult to explain if portfolio planning could be used only for one purpose, since the problems and priorities of top management tend to change and evolve over time, creating a need for many managerial tools and approaches. While portfolio planning does not provide an approach to all management problems, it can be applied to enough different and recurring issues to justify its long-term presence in many corporations.

The several uses of portfolio planning underscore the important role the CEO can and should play in determining the objectives the approach is to accomplish. In all of the companies studied, the use made of portfolio planning was the result of a conscious choice made by the chief executive. None of the CEOs interviewed indicated they used portfolio planning simply because they wanted to try a new planning approach. Instead they all explained, usually in historical terms and with reference to financial constraints and administrative considerations, the problem or problems they were trying to solve when they first adopted or later modified the use of portfolio planning. Indeed it is quite likely that portfolio planning has persisted precisely because CEOs have been able to use it in a variety of ways that meet their different objectives for their companies.

Portfolio planning, then, can be used for several purposes: to facilitate the allocation of resources, to improve the quality of business unit strategic plans, and to improve top management's understanding of the business units and of the overall corporate portfolio. The approach can be applied to affect either corporate or business strategy, but has little impact on institutional strategy. One of the crucial jobs of the chief executive is to determine the purpose for which portfolio planning is to be used and to assure that the use is consistent with the forces shaping strategic decision making. Just because several companies all report that they follow the portfolio approach to strategic planning does not mean they all use the technique for the same purpose or in the same way.

As discussed in the next two chapters, the use of portfolio planning techniques poses a variety of organizational issues. Significantly, the ways companies deal with these issues can be closely linked to the purpose and use they make of portfolio planning.

5

Defining Business Units

No matter which of the three purposes portfolio planning is to serve, its use inevitably poses a number of distinct organizational issues and dilemmas. In all of the companies studied, a recurring set of organizational issues could be identified. Of these, the problems of defining business units and of establishing their reporting relationships not only are the first issues managers confront but also are probably the most important in terms of shaping the relevance and impact of the portfolio approach to strategic planning.[1]

According to the theory of portfolio planning, the designation of strategic business units (SBUs) and their reporting relationships are straightforward. SBUs are identified by determining the unique sets of activities in a company that correspond to distinct markets, industries, and competitors. For resource allocation and planning purposes, all SBUs report directly to the CEO, who reviews SBU plans and makes resource allocation trade-offs among them. Despite the staightforward nature of these prescriptions, most companies experience considerable difficulty in designating, interrelating, and aggregating SBUs, and they have to consider a range of technical, administrative, and resource allocation issues when making these choices.

TECHNICAL ISSUES

The technical criteria commonly used to designate business units are summarized in the planning manual of one of the companies studied in the third phase of the research:

> *Strategic business units are a group of services/products having a common set of customers, a common set of competitors, a common technology/approach, and common critical success factors.*

In many cases, application of these criteria is uncomplicated and leads to significant improvements in planning. James Ferguson, CEO of General Foods, described how the identification of SBUs had improved strategic planning in his company:

> *We used to have several of what I would call "mini-businesses" sitting in different parts of the company. For example, our various dessert businesses were spread among two or three divisions, and the same was true of our beverage businesses. The reasons for this were largely historic in nature, having to do with when various businesses were acquired.*
>
> *The SBU concept provided a marvelous reason and rationale to combine these clearly related, but isolated, businesses into single SBUs. This enabled us to think about each of those businesses in enough detail, as one entity, to develop meaningful strategies and to allocate resources in a sensible manner.*

While many of the companies studied reported benefits similar to the ones identified by Ferguson, most also indicated that it was extremely difficult to designate some of their SBUs. At General Electric, for example, almost two years were needed to define all of the SBUs: Whereas about 80% of the SBU designations could be readily agreed on, the remaining 20% required considerable deliberation. Fred Borch, GE's CEO from 1963 to 1972, predicted these problems when he introduced the SBU concept to GE managers in May 1970:

I can assure you that we are going to have a lot of argument on what are going to be strategic business units. Probably none of the SBUs is truly going to meet all of the criteria. Let me give you an example. You would quickly say that if ever there were two businesses that had absolutely no relationship to each other, they would be Appliance and TV on the one hand, and the Space Group on the other. But let me remind you that because the Space Group gets involved with housing, we've got a sharp conflict right there. Therefore, the creation of the strategic business unit is going to be a judgmental decision.[2]

In addition to the problem of overlapping boundaries that Borch refers to, another difficulty is that often the various criteria suggest different SBU designations. For example, since washing machines and dishwashers serve very different purposes and are not substitutes for each other, it would be logical for each to be considered a separate business unit. Washing machines and dishwashers, however, face the same competitors, are distributed through the same channels, and use similar technologies; in this sense, they are part of one SBU.* When the criteria suggest different definitions, the task of designating SBUs is no longer a straightforward one but requires considerable judgment as to which criteria provide the proper basis for planning for future competition.

Even when the criteria do not conflict, problems can arise in defining the scope of a market. For example, a company that has a division producing metal cans can designate metal cans an SBU. It may, however, also want to define the business more broadly to include paper, glass, and plastic containers and to designate one SBU for all divisions competing in the packaging business. Or it may wish to take an opposite course, dividing its metal can division into two separate SBUs—one for aluminum cans and another for tin-plate cans. These problems in defining the scope of business units are extremely common and were experienced by all of the companies studied.

*General Electric had this situation and has designated all major appliances as one strategic business unit.

Finally, it is important to note that designation of SBUs cannot and should not be a one-time activity. This is because the technical criteria are often difficult to apply and because industry and competitive conditions often change in ways that necessitate changes in SBU designations. For example, a segment within an SBU may develop a distinct enough technology, or its market may become sufficiently large with enough new competitors, to justify the designation of the segment as a new and separate SBU. In other cases, the distinctions between some SBUs may blur over time, requiring their consolidation into a single SBU. Whatever the case, the important point is that even when SBU designation involves only technical criteria, top managers still have to exercise considerable judgment in applying the criteria and must remain alert to the need to redefine some of their SBUs periodically.

ADMINISTRATIVE ISSUES

In addition to requiring resolution of difficult technical questions, the designation of business units requires consideration of several important administrative issues. These issues are seldom mentioned in most discussions of portfolio planning, yet in the companies studied they were key considerations in defining SBUs.

The first of these issues is the amount of time the CEO has to interact with the SBUs. For in addition to conducting informal reviews, most CEOs schedule annual one-day formal reviews of all SBU strategic plans and spend considerable time on resource allocation decisions relating to the business units. These activities can place a tremendous burden on the already crowded schedule of most chief executives. Reginald Jones, General Electric's CEO from 1973 to 1981, explained how he approached this problem:

> Right from the start of SBU planning in 1972, the vice chairmen and I tried to review each of the forty-three SBU plans in great

detail. This was a considerable improvement from the 200 so-called business plans that we previously received from the depart-ments. That was impossible, and it was still a struggle when we got down to the forty-three strategic plans. This effort took untold hours and placed a tremendous burden on us.

You can't appreciate what I was up against. I don't believe in being remote and unapproachable, so I always tried to know what was going on in the operations. And now I was also getting over forty strategic plans a year. Each of them came in a three-ring binder several inches thick. And you can't read and understand one of those in the course of just one evening.

After a while I began to realize that no matter how hard we would work, we could not achieve the necessary in-depth understanding of the forty-odd SBU plans. Somehow the review burden had to be carried on more shoulders, and that's when we went to sectors. It was at that point that I could sit down and in great depth go through the six sector strategic plans and comprehend them thoroughly.

The time constraint of the CEO is one administrative problem that many companies have had to take into account when desig-nating SBUs. In very large and diverse companies, this nearly always means either reducing the number of SBUs from the num-ber suggested by only technical factors or creating additional levels of organization (e.g., groups or sectors) between the CEO and the SBUs. The head of planning at the Dexter Corporation indicated why Dexter placed an upper limit on the number of its SBUs:

We wanted no more than thirty business segments for the whole corporation—no more than five or six per division. Otherwise, we'd just have too many things to worry about.

A similar, very dramatic, example comes from the experiences of Union Carbide, which in 1975 proudly announced in its annual report that the company had identified and was intensely re-viewing the activities of over 150 SBUs. Within two years and with much less fanfare, that number was reduced to fewer than 40.

In contrast, General Electric has had roughly the same number of SBUs since it first introduced portfolio planning in the early 1970s. However, a new level of organization—sectors—was established to review the SBUs, which are now much larger and more diverse than they were when they were first created.

The capacity of a company's operating units to prepare strategic plans is another administrative factor that gets weighed when SBUs are being defined. Doing the background research and analysis to prepare an in-depth strategic plan takes a great deal of time. When the necessary time is not spent, the resulting plan is not grounded in a realistic assessment of market and competitive conditions, and strategic planning on the basis of such analysis can become meaningless. The administrative issue that this often poses is whether it is better to get 20 well-researched SBU plans than 50 mediocre plans, even if the number of distinct businesses that a company competes in is 50, not 20.

The limited capacity to do strategic planning was one of the major pitfalls of long-range planning at General Electric prior to 1972, when plans were prepared by all 180 GE departments. These plans were of questionable quality and, as Fred Borch noted, "It was amazing the company ran as well as it did with the planning that was being done or not being done at various operating levels." Not only did the designaton of 43 SBUs focus limited planning resources, but the additional requirement that each SBU hire one full-time planner assured that at least one man-year of effort went into the preparaton of each SBU strategic plan.

The need to take account of limited internal capabilities to do planning when designating SBUs was also evident at two of the companies studied later in the research. At one, 25 SBUs that corresponded to distinct markets had been identified, but top management was disappointed with the quality of the plans that were being produced. Because of the company's inexperience with strategic planning, it then designated seven much larger SBUs that would be staffed to prepare meaningful strategic plans. The result was a marked improvement in the quality of planning from the perspective of both corporate and SBU management. At the other company that had only recently diversified from a single business, the CEO described a similar situation:

> It does us no good to have someone say that we are really in fifteen businesses, because there is no way that we could plan for that many. Instead we need good plans for our three to five major activities.

The combination of limited capacity to do strategic planning and time constraints of the CEO often means that companies limit the number of their SBUs. Rather than identifying SBUs to correspond to the distinct markets that a company serves, *a more realistic prescription is to identify the limited number of important business entities that can command top management's time and interest and the company's capacity to focus attention.* Further evidence of the importance of limiting SBUs to a manageable number comes from the survey of *Fortune* 1000 companies, which found that the mean number of SBUs was 30 and that the number showed little variance related to the size of the company.[3] Given the tremendous range in the size and diversity of *Fortune* 1000 companies,* the consistency in the number of SBUs can best be explained by the importance of designating a manageable and understandable number of business units.

A final administrative issue that surfaces in the designation of business units is whether SBUs should correspond to existing organizational units. While it is possible to establish business units only on the basis of correspondence to distinct markets, this approach presents several organizational problems. For example, the Dexter Corporation, with the help of the Boston Consulting Group, first designated 16 business units, many of which did not correspond to operating units. As described by Dexter's head of planning, problems were experienced in getting managers to deal and identify with the new business units:

---

*In 1982, the sales of the *Fortune* 1000 companies ranged from a low of $122 million to a high of over $100 billion.

*We had gotten into some traps with the BCG-defined business segments. They weren't traps that we understood at the time. But as we went along **people became less and less interested because the segments were meaningless to them.***

To correct this problem, Dexter's management redefined business units that corresponded closely to the existing organization. The new criteria for defining SBUs were described as follows:

*We wanted the segments we picked to be **something people could associate with, segments that people could identify and were familiar with.** We wanted to avoid some of the traps we'd gotten into with BCG-defined segments.*

At General Electric, where SBUs differ greatly in size and may correspond to a department, a division, or a group, all of the SBUs still correspond to ongoing organizational units. At times, of course, GE and other companies have had to create new operating organizational units to correspond with SBUs. But the important point is that none of the companies studied chose to designate SBUs that had or would have no counterpart in the operating organization. The reason for this is that it is very hard to implement a strategy that does not tie directly to someone's area of responsibility in the organization. As one of the CEOs put it, "If it's worth having a strategy for a business, then you better have an organization that can implement it." Further confirmation of this point is provided in the survey of *Fortune* 1000 companies, in which only 7% of the companies reported that they designated any SBUs that did not correspond to operating units.[4]

RESOURCE ALLOCATION ISSUES

The designation of business units also raises important questions about the level at which resources are allocated. Typically it is assumed that the CEO, in conjunction with other members of top management, will make resource allocation trade-offs among the

SBUs. But as we have already seen, often the chief executive does not have the time, capacity, or inclination to become sufficiently familiar with all of the SBUs to make difficult resource allocation choices.

When this occurs, companies will often allocate resources in a two-tier process, first to intermediate levels of the organization, which in turn allocate resources to the business units. At several of the companies studied, SBU strategies were reviewed and resource allocation trade-offs were made at levels below the CEO. This was particularly the case at Dexter, where each division was required to maintain a balanced portfolio of businesses. Even though the five or six SBUs within each division had their plans and capital expenditure requests reviewed at the corporate level, each division was required to have a balanced cash flow. Consequently the divisions first allocated capital to their SBUs before they sought approvals for specific SBU capital requests. At Uniroyal, corporate management allocated different amounts of capital to its groups, which in turn allocated resources to the SBUs. Joe Flannery, Uniroyal's CEO, explained how his managers perceived this two-tier process:

> Our group vice presidents and their staffs see themselves as dividing one big pie and allocating resources to the SBUs within their groups. This resource allocation process within the groups is very visible and well understood. Even though resources are also allocated by corporate management to the groups, most of our managers understand resource allocation more in terms of trade-offs within their group, rather than within the entire company.

This two-tier approach to resource allocation can be achieved by the establishment of intermediate levels of organization, as at Dexter and Uniroyal, or by the definition of business units that are actually aggregates of several business segments.* An example of the latter approach is that of the Norton Company which had 30

---

*Some companies use both approaches, large SBUs and intermediate levels, to accomplish two-tier allocation.

SBUs, most of which consist of several of what they call "sub-strategic business units." This approach is far from uncommon, as indicated by the fact that almost 60% of the companies in the *Fortune 1000* survey establish and allocate resources to business units that are composed of business segments.[5] Decisions about resource allocation to these segments are made in turn by the business units. While there are many reasons for this practice that will be discussed later in this chapter and in the next, here it is important to note that, to the extent the CEO is willing to have resource allocation undertaken at lower levels in the organization, SBUs can be defined as larger units than those suggested by an analysis only of the company's distinct markets.

RESOLVING THE ISSUES

The way a company resolves the technical, administrative, and resource allocation issues involved in defining business units is of tremendous importance in how it uses portfolio planning and develops business strategies. While numerous issues need consideration, two of the most pervasive are whether many narrowly defined SBUs or fewer larger units should be designated, and whether resources should be allocated directly to the SBUs or via a two-tier process (in which resources are allocated to the SBUs by an intermediate level of organization or in which the SBUs allocate resources to business segments). The experiences of the companies studied suggest that these two choices are best resolved by a consideration of the use to which portfolio planning is being put, the forces that are shaping strategy, and the business strategies of the SBUs.

As shown in Table 5.1, for companies that use portfolio planning to allocate resources, the most sensible procedure is to define as many business units as a technical analysis suggests and to have the CEO allocate resources directly to each SBU. This approach gives corporate management the greatest ability to control where resources are being spent. It would be inconsistent with

TABLE 5.1.   RELATIONSHIPS BETWEEN MAJOR USES
OF PORTFOLIO PLANNING AND IDEAL NUMBER OF STRATEGIC
BUSINESS UNITS (SBUs) AND TYPE OF RESOURCE
ALLOCATION PROCESS

Use of Portfolio Planning	Number of SBUs Chosen	Type of Resource Allocation Process
Improvement in resource allocation	Many	Direct
Better understanding of business units and of overall corporate portfolio	Few	Two-tier
Improvement in SBU planning	Many	Two-tier

this use of portfolio to allocate resources to fewer, larger SBUs, because quite likely these large SBUs would in turn allocate resources to their business segments.

When portfolio planning is used to provide corporate management with an understanding of its business units and of the overall corporate portfolio, business units can usually be defined broadly and resources allocated via a two-tier process. This is because broad SBU definitions are usually sufficient to provide management with a rudimentary understanding of its portfolio of businesses and because top management does not want to get involved in detailed and direct resource allocation.

Finally, when portfolio planning is used to improve the quality of business unit planning, it makes sense to define many small SBUs and to allocate resources via a two-tier process. In this way, top management does not concern itself as much with resource allocation as with assuring that each of its many SBUs has developed the best possible strategy for its specific business. An example of this approach is that of the Dexter Corporation, which defines SBUs extremely narrowly so that detailed strategies are developed for each of the specialty markets the company competes in, but which allocates resources to these SBUs in a two-tier process.

Despite the straightforward nature of the prescriptions presented in Table 5.1, it would be naive to conclude that the choices of number of SBUs and type of resource allocation process could be resolved by considering only the purpose for which portfolio planning is being used. In most companies the choices are confounded because portfolio planning is serving more than one purpose and because the forces that shape strategic decision making also have a significant effect.

For example, a company facing tight financial constraints is well advised to allocate resources directly to many SBUs. When financial resources are more plentiful, however, a two-tier approach, with fewer SBUs or with intermediate levels of management, is usually more appropriate. Similarly, a CEO who chooses to manage outcomes by direct involvement in the substance of important decisions will want to allocate resources directly, while another CEO who prefers to manage processes by assuring that all options have been considered and all affected parties consulted would be more inclined to adopt a two-tier approach. The capabilities of operating management also affect the advisability of pursuing a two-tier approach to resource allocation. As operating managers become more capable of preparing sophisticated strategic plans, a two-tier approach can be pursued with little effect on quality and with the advantage of resource allocation decisions being made close to the level where they are implemented.

The experiences of the General Electric Company illustrate how both the purpose of using portfolio planning and the forces shaping strategic decision making influence the designation of SBUs and the type of resource allocation process. When GE introduced portfolio planning in 1972, the company had a great need to address resource allocation problems and for the operating units to develop the ability to do strategic planning. The result was that 43 SBUs were named and that each one reported directly to the CEO for review and resource allocation purposes. By 1977, GE's allocation of resources had greatly improved, the capabilities of the organization to do sophisticated planning had increased considerably, and the purpose of using portfolio planning had shifted from just resource allocation to inclusion of the other two uses as well. Moreover, GE's CEO, Reg Jones, was shifting his management approach from the management of outcomes to the management of processes. Consistent with these changes, a two-tier approach to resource allocation was adopted, and the CEO reviewed only the six sector plans instead of all 43 SBU plans.

Finally, it is important to acknowledge the important effects the designation of business units can have on the strategies those units adopt and the organizational problems the units face. While the latter are discussed in the next chapter, here we can note how the choices influence business unit strategy. For example, General Electric's decision to create one SBU for all of its medical systems businesses has led that SBU to expand its product line to include new diagnostic imaging techniques, making it a pioneer in the development of computed tomography scanners and nuclear magnetic resonance equipment. If, on the other hand, the SBU had been defined solely as a supplier of x-ray equipment, which was its original product base, there is some likelihood that the company would not have moved as aggressively into new product areas.

Another example of the strategic significance of SBU definition comes from the General Motors Corporation. For years automotive strategic planning at General Motors had been carried out by the five car divisions: Chevrolet, Pontiac, Buick, Oldsmobile, and Cadillac. As the strategies of these divisions increasingly addressed only the middle to upper part of the automotive market, however, it became apparent that the company was not developing a strategy for competing in the small-car market. The solution to this problem was the reorganization, announced early in 1984, of GM's automotive operations into two divisions, one having responsibility for small cars and the other for large cars. This restructuring of General Motors should greatly improve the company's ability to plan for the small-car segment, something that was previously lacking.[6] To the extent that the automotive market consists of other segments, such as station wagons, sports cars, and luxury cars, however, the new organization will not assure that specific strategies are developed to compete in them.

The purpose of these examples is not to develop SBU designations for General Motors or General Electric. It is to illustrate that *the definition of an SBU can affect the way the managers of the unit perceive and compete in their business.* This suggests that SBU strategy, which is usually considered a product of the planning process, must be taken into account in the definition of SBUs in the first place. This tight linkage, or reciprocal relationship, between an SBU's definition and its strategy is consistent with Burgelman's findings:

> *Structure and strategy thus exist in a reciprocal relationship to each other. Depending on which part of the strategic process is observed, both "structure follows strategy" and "strategy follows structure" can be correct propositions.[7]*

That the definition of an SBU can influence its strategy is one of the many reasons why designation of business units is not only the first step in portfolio planning but is also the most important. It is precisely *because* portfolio planning techniques pay close attention to such variables as market share and market growth that a careful definition of the market being considered is essential. General Motors' share of the mid-size-car market is very high, but the company is less dominant in the total automotive market and is a weak competitor in the small-car segment. How the company defines its SBUs will shape management's perception of its competitive position and will have a tremendous impact on the strategy of each SBU and of the total company as well. Derek Abell reached a similar conclusion in his study of these issues:

> *To give paramount attention to a company's market share and growth strategy within a particular market is begging the question if the definition of the activity within which that share is to be measured is not explicitly resolved.[8]*

Two very important conclusions suggested by this analysis are that the use of portfolio planning techniques requires careful attention to how business units are defined and that top management should be prepared to redefine its business units periodically. SBU definitions probably should change simply because markets evolve, new technologies emerge, financial constraints change, and new strategies are developed. New definitions of some of a company's SBUs are essential to keeping abreast of changing market and internal conditions. Equally important, evolving organizational capabilities and business strategies often necessitate a change in SBU designations. Far from being a preliminary first step that precedes the more important parts of portfolio planning, the designation of SBUs is an ongoing activity that is inextricably linked to how portfolio planning techniques arc used and to their ultimate impact and utility.

6

Organizational Consequences
and Responses

Ever since diversified corporations
first appeared in this country in the early 1920s, their top managers have been dealing with the dilemma of how much autonomy to grant company divisions and how to structure corporate-divisional relations. Even Alfred Sloan, who is credited with developing General Motors' decentralized organization, recognized some of these conflicts when he described the principles on which GM's organization was based:

> The language is contradictory, and that it is contradictory is the crux of the matter. In point 1, I maximize decentralization of divisional operations. . . . In point 2, I proceed to limit the responsibility of divisional chief executives.[1]

Despite the many advances in management practice since the 1920s, the inherent conflicts (or contradictions) in management of a diversified and decentralized company remain. Vancil's conclusion, after surveying the practices of 300 decentralized companies in the mid-1970s, is remarkably similar to Sloan's:

> In contrast to the clean lines of functional authority in a central-
> ized organization, decentralization produces contradictory, am-
> biguous roles for profit center managers — and intentionally
> so. . . . The benefits of managing [this] ambiguity are apparently
> worth the costs.[2]

Given this background, it would be surprising if the use of
portfolio planning techniques did not reflect some of the dilemmas inherent in management of a diversified company and pose
some of its own ambiguous and contradictory organizational
issues. Indeed this is the case. The experiences of the companies
that were studied point to some very positive organizational outcomes of portfolio planning and to other very serious organizational consequences that require considerable top management
attention.

POSITIVE CONSEQUENCES

In many companies, portfolio planning helps to clarify top management's expectations for its divisions. This is because the development of strategic mandates and resource allocation guidelines
can provide an opportunity for corporate and divisional management to discuss and reach common expectations. Robert Cushman, the Norton Company's chief executive from 1971 to 1980,
explained this benefit:

> Within a year of beginning to use portfolio planning, I was able to
> achieve a cohesiveness among our managers that we had never
> had before. For the first time, everyone knew how their objectives
> fit into the overall needs of the company and the direction in which
> we were headed.

Although all forms of strategic planning require a dialogue
about divisional goals, too often these discussions are so far ranging and general that they are of little value. The use of portfolio
planning can improve these discussions by focusing attention on

a few key items, most notably on investment plans and market share.

Closely related to this, portfolio planning legitimatizes having a different set of expectations for each division. A high-level executive who was interviewed during the first phase of this research commented:

> Before, we had the same requirements for each division. They were all supposed to grow 10% a year and earn a 15% return. We now recognize that our divisions should have very different goals depending on their maturity and strength. This has made it easier for us to understand our businesses and has also made it easier on our division managers, who no longer have to meet an arbitrary target.

Don MacKinnon, president of CIBA-GEIGY's U.S. operations, elaborated on this point:

> We have 28 SBUs in our company and each one has a different role to play. These range from **pillar businesses** which are highly profitable and get highest priority for resources, to **small but beautiful businesses** that are earning a high return but that we choose not to invest in, to **cash generator businesses.**
>
> The different goals for these businesses have liberated our division managers each to play a vital role for the corporation while pursuing different and more realistic objectives. For example, we have some cash generator businesses that used to be considered losers when their profitability and growth were compared with other divisions. With portfolio planning, these businesses are given a different set of objectives that deal with cash generation, and today they are considered winners.

Another benefit of portfolio planning is that it fosters an organizational structure based on distinct businesses. At General Foods, this benefit was realized by combining small, clearly related but isolated businesses into single SBUs. At CIBA-GEIGY, the functionally organized divisions were reorganized on a product line basis. Don MacKinnon explained:

> For a long time, all five of our divisions had been functionally organized. I had felt for a while that this structure made us concentrate too much on the functions of the business—manufacturing, marketing, etc.—and not enough on our markets.
>
> When we introduced portfolio planning, each of our divisions had to view itself as consisting of several SBUs. As a result, within two years, all of our divisions had reorganized on an SBU basis.

A final organizational benefit of portfolio planning is that it legitimatizes consideration of divestiture as a valid strategic alternative rather than as an admission of failure. Given the stigma that often comes from association with a division that is sold or liquidated, this is a significant benefit of portfolio planning. An executive at General Electric described how portfolio planning legitimatized divestitures at that company:

> The planning system was just another tool that enabled a manager to face up to certain inevitabilities. Prior to this, we had really operated with a "floating J curve." In other words, businesses would forecast two or three years of flat or declining profitability, but then all of the numbers would point upwards. What Jones [CEO] was able to do with the computer business* and what strategic planning revealed was that the floating J curve was a fantasy.

Jack Welch, GE's current chief executive, pointed to the same benefits of portfolio planning when he said that "we have to get used to the idea that disengaging does not mean bad people or bad management. It's a bad situation and we can't afford to tie up good resources—both in terms of dollars and people—by chasing them."

In terms of its positive organizational effects, then, portfolio planning can help to clarify top management's expectations of divisional performance. It legitimatizes having different performance standards for each division, it fosters an organizational structure based on distinct businesses, and it facilitates divestiture of some of a company's businesses.

---

*In May 1970, General Electric sold its computer business to Honeywell. See Chapter 10 for a detailed account of this event.

NEGATIVE CONSEQUENCES

The use of portfolio planning techniques is usually associated with labeling of the strategy of each division and with establishment of controls and incentives to reinforce the mandated strategy. While these practices can have some of the positive consequences just noted, they can also have some very negative consequences when they lead to unfortunate self-fulfilling prophecies, to undue conservatism in business and investment planning, and to an overreliance on the inputs of staff planners.

Most of the self-fulfilling prophecies associated with portfolio planning originate in the management of mature cash cow businesses. Memorex provides an excellent example of this phenomenon.* In the late 1960s, Chief Executive Laurence Spitters decided to manage Memorex's highly successful computer tape business as a cash cow. He explained his thinking in terms that reflect the theory of portfolio management:

> Computer tape operations will face declining profit margins as the tape industry develops the competitive conditions of a mature industry. Reduced profit margins may be countered periodically by new product improvements, but these will not change the long-term results.

In managing Memorex, Spitters cut off investment funds to the computer tape business and spent lavishly on the targeted high-growth divisions in the disk pack, disk drive, and computer mainframe fields. The managers of these growth divisions were offered very large bonuses and were given considerable latitude to conduct their businesses as they saw fit. The managers in the tape division, on the other hand, were offered little in the way of bonuses and had their performance tightly monitored by corporate management. Within a few years these policies led to low morale and high turnover in the tape division, with the result that Memorex lost its number 1 position in the computer tape market.

*See Chapter 11 for more information on Memorex.

This example, while dramatic, is by no means atypical. In all of the companies studied, managers could cite examples of decisions to harvest businesses that inadvertently led, or nearly led, to the abandonment of those businesses.* For example, at General Foods, Jim Ferguson cited several unfortunate examples:

> We had major problems in trying to run our mature businesses for cash flow. My managers would ask me, "Don't you want us to think about growth opportunities for our business?" My response would be, "Yes, **but**." In other words, I would agree with them, but my underlying message would be that their real objective was to produce cash for the corporation. In retrospect, the concept of cash-cow and mature business got in the way of both growth and innovation.

> Coffee is a good case in point. Naturally, with declining consumption, our coffee business had been classified as a cash-cow or maintenance product. In point of fact, however, this is a very volatile and dynamic business. For example, in recent years, with the advent of automatic coffee makers in the home, there has been a lot of activity in the ground coffee market to develop new varieties of ground coffees. We didn't necessarily miss these opportunities, but I believe we were a little late and not as aggressive in pursuing them because of the cash-cow concept.

Occasionally, the business press has also reported such problems, as in the following account of Timex's difficulties in managing its mechanical watch division:

> Timex's guiding theory held that the outlook of makers of mechanical watches was the opposite of what success in the electronic-watch business required. People who had managed Timex's mechanical-watch operation, therefore, should be quarantined off to run their own business—into the ground, ultimately—while

---

*Harvesting refers to managing a business so as to maximize its ability to generate positive cash flows. While in theory harvesting should not preclude new investment that would sustain a business's ability to generate cash, in practice such investments, because of their short-term negative effect on cash flow, are often foregone. It is this practice that can lead to the abandonment of the business.

electronics hotshots should be hired to produce the company's future.... That sales of windup watches would inexorably decline, all hands agreed; how quickly was the only question. To manage the shrinkage properly, the trick was to keep reducing productive capacity below the level of potential sales, milking the business for profits as it grew smaller, while channeling the capital released from it into digital watches or other new ventures. As for slowing the decline with advertising and product upgrading to keep profits flowing as long as possible, you'd think that would go without saying.

*But spending support was choked off right away. "We started treating the mechanical as if it had only hours to live," says a 1981 internal company memo. As a result, adds a former employee, "we allowed our **only** product to die."[3] [emphasis in the original.]*

In addition to the problem of underinvesting, it is difficult to inspire commitment and enthusiasm in a business whose major objective is to produce large cash flows for other SBUs to invest. That is, the decision to harvest a business can lead to a self-fulfilling prophecy wherein the decision leads to tighter controls and less autonomy, which lead to poor performance and the resignations of key managers, which lead possibly to the disposition of the business unit. A group vice president of a large industrial company, whom I interviewed during the first phase of the research, explained how he had experienced this problem:

Two of the divisions that report to me are in very sluggish industries. In one case we have been able to develop more original strategies, have the employees all fired up, and are making a good return. But I have to fight to keep the corporate planners from giving their view of the situation. In the other division, the notion that it is a dog has been allowed to permeate down from the top. I feel there are some original things we could do there, but it's impossible to get anyone at the division very excited to try something new. Eventually we will probably sell or liquidate the division.

Although a less common problem, the use of portfolio planning techniques can also have negative consequences on businesses that are targeted for growth. At Memorex, for example, such divisions did grow rapidly at first, but then they evinced disturbing signs of loss of control: high inventory levels, high warranty costs, and frequent complaints about new products. Eventually some of these growth divisions began operating at a loss.

The negative consequence of portfolio planning for rapidly growing divisions, then, is that its use can foster such strong backing from enthusiastic corporate managers that often there is too little interest in scrutinizing and controlling the businesses earmarked for growth. Rapidly growing businesses typically face numerous organizational problems as they attempt to expand their organization and maintain control, and lack of corporate-level involvement often exacerbates the problems.[4] Overexuberance can also lead to less thorough review of investment proposals and to making acquisitions in growth areas at such high prices that the company is unlikely ever to earn a satisfactory return on the investments.[5]

When portfolio planning leads both to the abandonment of previously healthy, albeit mature, divisions and to lack of control in a rapidly growing division, the results can be disastrous. Indeed this was the case at Memorex, which sustained substantial losses. Fortunately, however, managers can take many actions to minimize these self-fulfilling prophecies.

In addition to the potential for leading to self-fulfilling prophecies, the use of portfolio planning can also have the negative effect of causing managers to become less expansionary and more conservative in developing strategy. As one CEO commented, "I certainly didn't intend for it to be this way, but we are now getting a lot fewer proposals to enter new businesses than when we started using the portfolio concept." While the reasons for this conservatism are developed in greater detail in the next chapter, here it is important to note that portfolio matrices are usually prepared only to evaluate a company's *existing* portfolio of businesses. With the ranking of existing businesses as its major purpose, it is not surprising that portfolio planning can cause new business opportunities to fall out of the purview of managers.

Closely related to this, the use of portfolio planning can sometimes lead to overreliance on the inputs of staff planners and to insufficient consideration of the views of operating managers. Jack Welch spoke of these problems shortly after he became General Electric's CEO:

> Our planning system was dynamite when we first put it in. The thinking was fresh; the form mattered little—the format got no points. It was idea-oriented. We then hired a head of planning and he hired two vice presidents and then he hired a planner, and the books got thicker and the printing got more sophisticated, and the covers got harder and the drawings got better. The meetings kept getting larger. Nobody can say anything with 16 or 18 people there.

Joe Flannery of Uniroyal voiced a similar sentiment when he told me that "after two years of doing portfolio planning I started to get concerned that the process of planning had become too onerous and in a sense had captured us. We were concentrating too much on analysis and not enough on specific decisions and implementation."

MANAGING THE PROS AND CONS

Companies can choose a number of approaches and modifications in the way they use portfolio planning to mitigate some of the technique's negative consequences and to maximize its benefits. Most of these approaches have been developed over time as companies have gained more experience with and have had to deal with some of the negative consequences. While these modifications and approaches take numerous forms, the companies studied here repeatedly faced five choices that greatly affected the organizational consequences of portfolio planning: (1) whether to label the strategies of the SBUs, (2) how to structure corporate-business unit relationships, (3) what attitude to take toward mature businesses, (4) whether to use a two-tier resource allocation process, and (5) how to structure the planning process.

Labeling Strategies of SBUs. The first choice that can affect the organizational consequences of portfolio planning is whether the strategy of each SBU should be given a specific label such as "star" or "cash cow." The assumption is often made that all companies that use portfolio planning follow this practice, but actually this is far from the case. For example, the Dexter Corporation intentionally does not label its business unit strategies. Dexter's president, Worth Loomis, explained that the reason for this is to avoid "motivational and political problems" that could hamper morale at the business unit level. Jim Ferguson of General Foods explained that he dropped labeling because of its negative effects on mature businesses:

> When we began using portfolio planning, we assigned each of our SBUs to specific categories. . . . Our use of these categories was not particularly successful, and after a few years we dropped them. We simply had too many difficulties in applying the concept, and the categories were hurting our more mature businesses. Without categories, we have been able to develop the attitude that these businesses can grow and innovate.

Dexter and General Foods are not isolated examples of companies that do not label their SBUs' strategies. Of the more than 300 companies that participated in Haspeslagh's survey of *Fortune 1000* companies, approximately one half did and one half did not explicitly label each SBU as belonging in a specific strategic category.[6]

The choice of whether to label SBU strategies provides corporate managers with an opportunity either to limit some of the negative organizational consequences of the portfolio approach or to emphasize some of its positive effects. In general, not labeling helps to avoid motivational problems and unfortunate self-fulfilling prophecies for harvest businesses, but it leaves top managers with the problem of finding other ways to communicate their expectations to these SBUs. On the other hand, labeling is a very direct way to clarify top management's expectations and to ensure that the SBUs understand the investment implications of their competitive and market situations. Because labeling is such a direct and blunt signal of top management's expectations, it also tends to tilt the balance between centralization and decentralization within a company toward greater centralization, while not labeling usually has the opposite effect. Explicitly labeling each SBU with a strategic category, then, provides top managers with a way to affect the organizational consequences of portfolio planning, and it also becomes a part of the way a company resolves the more basic dilemma of how much autonomy to give its operating units.

Structuring of Corporate Business Relationships. Another choice that affects the consequences of portfolio planning is how top managers structure their relationships with the SBUs. After collecting data on the performance of 69 SBUs in 12 companies, White concluded that corporate-business unit relationships are a major determinant of business unit performance:

> Corporate management can have as much impact on a business unit's performance by attending to its administrative ties to head-quarters as they can by managing according to detailed strategic portfolio analyses.[7]

In examining the impact of autonomy, line responsibility, and incentive compensation on business unit performance, White found that many of the guidelines suggested by portfolio theory are inappropriate.[8] For example, he found that business units competing in growth markets often require more attention from corporate managers than those competing in mature industries. This finding is the opposite of what is typically suggested by portfolio planning advocates, yet, as shown in Table 6.1, for mature business units (those in stable market environments), high autonomy is associated with considerably faster sales growth than is low autonomy, but under either high or low autonomy return on investment (ROI) is very comparable. On the other hand, for SBUs competing in dynamic environments,* high autonomy is again

*Dynamic environments have frequent product introductions, sweeping technologic changes, and fluctuating market shares between competitors; stable environments have the opposite characteristics.

TABLE 6.1.   RATE OF SALES GROWTH AND RETURN ON INVESTMENT
(ROI) ACCORDING TO DEGREE OF AUTONOMY AND THE VOLATILITY
OF THE BUSINESS ENVIRONMENT

Environment of Business (no. of observations)	Rate of Sales Growth (%)		ROI (%)	
	Low Autonomy	High Autonomy	Low Autonomy	High Autonomy
Dynamic (35)	5.9	12.0	23.3	14.3
Stable (34)	3.7	6.8	22.7	20.9
Total sample (69)	4.9	9.0	23.0	18.2

associated with more rapid sales growth but also with significantly lower ROI than is low autonomy.

These conclusions are quite consistent with the experiences of
the companies studied here: The low autonomy given to cash-cow
SBUs often led to very unfavorable results, and the loose control
of growth SBUs did facilitate sales growth but sometimes at the
expense of profits. General Electric has avoided this latter trap
by paying very close attention to its growth businesses and to
the managers running them. Jack Welch described how GE ac-
complishes this:

> We have a section of our manpower books on ventures. What are
> the 12 embryo businesses in your sector that are being fueled by
> what 12 people?. . . By having high visibility on a dozen people. . .
> we get a chance to look at how they perform.

In a sense, the managers of business units competing in dynamic environments have so many options that they are quite
likely to benefit from the involvement of corporate managers. Too
often when left to their own devices, these business unit managers
tend to pursue sales opportunities rather than profitability. Corporate managers can often play a useful role by stepping in,
tightening the reins a bit, and ensuring that sales growth is balanced with profitability.

Closely related to this, corporate managers can influence the
organizational consequences of portfolio planning by the way

they compensate their business unit managers. White's data on the compensation practices in 12 companies suggest that, unfortunately, top managers have difficulty in establishing appropriate incentives for managers of business units competing in stable environments. Even though the top managers of these companies indicated that they tried to offer the same degree of incentive compensation to all of their SBU managers, the data in Table 6.2 show that, regardless of their ROI, the managers of units with high sales growth were rewarded better than their counterparts in slow-growth businesses. While it is possible that higher levels of base compensation may offset lower levels of incentive compensation, the experiences of the companies studied suggest that, although top managers talk about rewarding the managers of mature businesses with high incentives, they often do not translate this idea into meaningful action. To overcome this problem, top managers need to devise specific incentives for each business unit rather than assume that one set of incentives will work for all growth businesses and another for all mature businesses. At Norton Company, for example, Robert Cushman used over 50 custom-tailored incentive plans. He explained that "no management task is more difficult than harvesting a business over a long period of time, and I had to assure that the managers who were given this task were well motivated and rewarded."

Attitude Toward Mature Businesses. Top managers can also affect the organizational consequences of portfolio planning by the attitude they take toward their mature businesses. Simply put,

TABLE 6.2. CASH BONUS IN RELATION
TO SALES GROWTH AND PROFITABILITY

Return on Investment	Real Sales Growth	
	Low	High
Low	12.3%[a]	15.5%
High	8.6%	22.7%

[a]Cash bonus as percentage of total compensation.

the attitude that these business units are dull laggards only increases the chance that morale in the unit will deteriorate, that market changes will not be recognized, and that the business eventually will be sold or liquidated. To combat this, it is important for top managers to develop the attitude that mature businesses may still require investment to remain competitive, that important changes requiring aggressive responses do occur in these markets, and that profitable mature businesses are an essential part of a company's portfolio. Worth Loomis described this attitude:

> *The secret of dealing with so-called harvest businesses is never to really harvest them, but in a sense to put them in idle. That way you are ready to put the business back in gear whenever an opportunity arises. My philosophy has never been that you have to get rid of a business just because it isn't growing. In fact, as long as the business is earning a higher return than your cost of capital, there's every reason to keep it.*

Jim Ferguson elaborated on this attitude and gave an example of its effects:

> *What we have learned is that concepts such as the product life cycle or portfolio analysis are very good in theory, but that they can get you into a lot of trouble if you really believe that what is theorized will actually happen. I have found it much more important to challenge our managers **to develop an attitude that we should make sure the theory will not come to pass.***

> *An example of where this attitude has paid off for us is in our dessert business, led by our very mature Jell-O product. Instead of accepting inevitable decline, the managers of this business have found opportunities to grow and innovate by developing entirely new lines of frozen dessert products and by improving existing products with the use of aspartame.*

A sector executive at General Electric described how his company had come to similar conclusions:

> *In the 1970s, we may not have invested enough in some of our mature businesses. We assumed that just because a business was in*

a slowly growing market it was not a very good business. Now we understand much better just how profitable a business can be even though its industry is only growing by two percent. We have redefined the cash cow concept and are now investing a lot of money in SBUs that we used to call cash cows.

To encourage a more positive attitude in mature units, some companies actually have begun to appoint their most aggressive managers to head these units. At several of the companies studied, top managers explained that this practice alone could lead to a revitalization, rather than the decline, of these businesses. The requirement that many companies (including Dexter and General Electric) have adopted—that all of their SBUs have either number 1 or 2 market share—can be another way to instill a positive attitude about mature SBUs. The reason for this is that the business units with high shares are typically slated to receive the investment funds they need to maintain their strong competitive positions, regardless of the growth of their market.

Resource Allocation.   Corporate management can also affect the organizational consequences of portfolio planning by the way business units are defined and resources are allocated. Typically, having larger SBUs and a two-tier resource allocation process minimizes the negative consequences by somewhat camouflaging the performance of mature businesses, which tends to leave them more time and resources to improve their performance, and by mitigating the chances that businesses will be abandoned. Moreover it is quite common for larger SBUs to manage themselves as portfolios of businesses, with the important benefits that resource allocation decisions are made closer to the businesses and that the overall SBU has a chance to reposition itself. Donald Melville, the current CEO of the Norton Company, explained why he tried to create large SBUs that allocate resources to their segments:

I like having our SBUs, and particularly the mature ones, large enough so that they contain some growth segments. Most of them look at themselves as a portfolio of businesses, and I encourage that. For example, one of the mature businesses has developed a strategy in which they think of themselves as consisting of seven or eight discrete businesses. Just this morning, I was meeting with them about an investment proposal for one of their businesses that has growth opportunities. I am encouraging them to spend the money. In this way, we have made it very acceptable for our mature SBUs to ask for money and have made things less onerous for them because they have a growth part of their business.

On the other hand, having lots of narrowly defined SBUs that are aggregated only at the corporate level tends to spotlight the performance of the SBUs. This usually ensures that mature businesses are harvested for cash, but it also runs the risk of leading to their abandonment. Interestingly, it may make sense to create smaller SBUs for rapidly growing, new businesses. Don Melville, for example, indicated that he favored this approach because it enabled him to keep close tabs and place the necessary controls on these emerging growth businesses.

Planning Process Structure.   Finally, the organizational consequences of portfolio planning can be affected by the planning process itself. For example, a process that rests heavily on the inputs of corporate staff executives and in which corporate management assigns labels and categories to each SBU is more likely to clarify top management's expectations, but it can also lead to serious motivational problems within the SBUs. As a result of these problems, many companies are placing much greater emphasis on the inputs of line managers. At General Electric, for example, the number of staff planners has been cut in half and responsibility for strategy has been given directly to the SBU general managers. Bill Marquard, CEO of American Standard, explained his approach to this issue:

We have a very small planning staff at the corporate level, and most of our planners have operating experience. Those who don't are exposed to our operations as part of their jobs. We also require our head of planning to sit in on our monthly operations reviews. In that way, the planner is able to make sure that his plans are developed with a practical in-depth understanding of what we are facing.

Similarly, many companies are finding that, after the first two or three years, during which the collection of considerable new data about markets and competitors is necessary, it is possible and even beneficial to reduce these requirements. Joe Flannery of Uniroyal explained:

> We used to spend too much time in our planning discussing issues and data that had no impact on what we were going to do. Today our planning process begins by identifying the key issues and decisions that each SBU faces. Our planning is then focused on determining what we should do about each of these issues. We are trying to collect only those data that help us to decide what to do and not to fill out forms and collect data for their own sake.

Resolving the Choices

How a company makes its choices on the issues just discussed depends on the purpose the CEO has in using portfolio planning and on the other forces that influence strategic decision making. For example, when portfolio planning is being used to facilitate divestitures and corporate restructuring and when financial resources are tightly constrained, a company is more likely to label the strategies of its SBUs, to be less patient with its mature units, and to control resource allocation to many smaller SBUs directly from the top of the corporation. When improvements in business unit planning or corporate understanding of the businesses is the major objective, there is less need to label the SBUs, to differentiate their rewards and controls, and to allocate resources directly to each business.

In terms of the forces shaping strategic decision making, companies facing tight financial constraints tend to pay less attention to the negative organizational consequences of portfolio planning, while companies with strong, independent divisions are more inclined to take steps to mitigate some of these consequences. Similarly, a CEO who prefers to manage outcomes is more likely to label SBU strategies and to be less sensitive to organizational consequences than a CEO who is inclined to manage decision processes.

The way a company deals with the organizational consequences of portfolio planning is also closely related to how strategy is developed within the company. For example, in a company where strategies emanate from the top, it is consistent for corporate management to assign strategic labels and categories to each of its SBUs and then to design a rigid set of incentives and controls for the units depending on their category. In a company where all managerial levels are involved in developing strategy, however, strategic labels may be the subject of serious analysis and debate between corporate and business unit management, and incentives may be tailored to the specific conditions facing each SBU. Even though both of these companies end up labeling the strategies of their business units, the decision-making processes leading to this choice are very different, and therefore it is much more likely that there will be negative organizational consequences in the first case than in the second.

Given the number of organizational issues posed by portfolio planning and the range of responses that companies can adopt to deal with them, it should not be surprising that the most striking thing about the companies studied here is that they all managed the issues posed by portfolio planning in their own unique ways. There were, of course, many similarities and patterns, but the more important point is that there was no one prescribed way for all companies to use and apply portfolio planning. The variety of possible approaches shows that the successful use of portfolio planning requires the CEO to understand the purpose the techniques are to serve and the financial and administrative constraints facing the company, and then to adapt and modify the use of portfolio planning to meet both personal needs and those of the organization.

The range of approaches companies can take to address the organizational consequences of portfolio planning should not overshadow the necessity of ensuring that the quality and capabilities of an SBU's management remain of paramount importance to top management. Virtually all of the CEOs who were interviewed commented on this point. Bill Marquard of American Standard expressed it this way:

The biggest weakness of the portfolio approach is that it doesn't account for the quality of your management. I like to say that a good management team can make a mediocre plan work. But you can never make a good plan work with poor management.

The major problems we have had with portfolio planning have come up when some of our people start to think that the numbers and the portfolio concept are King. The result is that, when they see some bad numbers or some bad indicators, their immediate reaction is to get out of the business. In my experience, good management can and should solve many of those problems.

Donald Melville of the Norton Company added the following:

I have never seen it mentioned in connection with portfolio planning, but I feel that the quality of management within your business is the ultimate indicator of your eventual success or failure. Our SBUs that have prospered . . . some of which required resuscitation . . . have done so because of the quality of their managements. No matter how a company approaches portfolio planning, a central part of my job must be to get the best possible people to run our businesses.

CONCLUSION

In this chapter and the previous one, we have discussed the practical day-to-day issues that managers face when using portfolio planning techniques in their organizations. In most discussions of portfolio planning these issues receive little, if any, attention. Yet far from being irrelevant, these implementation issues are at the heart of the problems managers face in trying to make portfolio planning and strategy work in their organizations. It is the ability to manage these issues effectively, rather than the sophistication of technical analyses, that distinguishes those companies able to use portfolio planning to move their companies forward from those whose experiences end in frustration or misfortune.

Portfolio planning cannot, and never was intended to, resolve all of the dilemmas inherent in running companies that are both diversified and decentralized. And using the techniques as if those dilemmas and problems do not exist or will disappear can have only negative consequences. Simply put, the development of experience curves, growth-share matrices, or 9-block grids is only one small part of the use of portfolio planning. As we shall see in the next chapter, effective use requires considerably more technical analysis than the mere application of techniques. Equally important, effective use of portfolio planning also requires the ability to anticipate and to manage its organizational consequences.

7
The Impact of Portfolio Planning on Strategy

Since portfolio planning was first introduced, many claims have been made about the impact the techniques have on the strategies that companies pursue. Determination of the precise impact has proved difficult, however, because of the problems of isolating the effects of portfolio planning from the other forces shaping strategy and because of the many definitions of strategy that are used. In this chapter, the data I collected throughout my research are analyzed in a way that takes account of these two problems. The impact of portfolio planning techniques on each of the three levels of strategy— business strategy, corporate strategy, and institutional strategy— is considered, as is the way the impact differs depending on the CEO's objective in using the approach and on the other forces that shape strategic decisions.

PORTFOLIO PLANNING AND BUSINESS STRATEGY

Chapter 1 discussed the use of portfolio planning techniques in the selection of strategic mandates or basic, overall market share and cash flow objectives for the business strategy of each unit in a company. The experiences of the companies studied suggest that, when used in this way, portfolio planning techniques have a mixed effect on business strategy; in some instances they are very helpful, while in others they are misleading.

Portfolio planning techniques can lead to inappropriate business strategies when it is assumed that high market share and the lowest possible costs are important in all industries and for all competitors within an industry. This assumption can lead to unnecessary and expensive share-building and cost-cutting efforts. This occurred at the Dexter Corporation's semiconductor molding powder business.* In 1974, this business was the subject of an intensive study by the Boston Consulting Group. The business had been experiencing difficulties, and BCG recommended that the unit attempt to improve its performance by building market share and developing standard molding powder products whose costs and prices could be lowered as the unit gained increasing experience and market share. While this recommendation is consistent with the emphasis portfolio planning techniques place on low costs and high market share, it does not correspond to competitive realities in the semiconductor molding powder industry, in which the product is only a small percentage of customers' total costs and in which, consequently, high-quality products and continual development of new products for each new generation of semiconductor devices are essential for competitive success. Thus a business strategy of producing low-cost, standard products was inappropriate for this SBU, and by 1978 the performance of Dexter's semiconductor molding powder business had shown little improvement.

Another problem in applying portfolio planning techniques to the development of business strategy is that the strategic mandates of portfolio planning define business strategy at too high a level of abstraction, overlooking crucial considerations and details. Simply put, a mandate to grow or to harvest is only one

*This situation is described in greater detail in Chapter 9.

objective for a business unit; it is not a complete business strategy that specifies the markets in which the unit will compete, the products that will be sold, their performance and price characteristics, the way in which they will be produced and distributed, and the method of financing. To the extent that portfolio planning encourages business strategy to become synonymous with market share and cash flow objectives, business strategies are likely to be incomplete and ineffectual. Jim Ferguson of General Foods explained:

> Our purpose in each of our businesses is to grow and to compete effectively. Cash flow is what you have as the result of a hard day or year of work. It is not the purpose of running a business.

A final problem can arise if it is assumed that an SBU's position on a portfolio grid cannot change over time. For while an important benefit of the portfolio planning approach is that it forces managers to come to terms with untenable competitive situations, the position of an SBU on the portfolio grid can often be improved by development of a new, creative business strategy. Reginald Jones, General Electric's CEO from 1972 to 1981, emphasized this point:

> If all of the SBUs are in the same position on the portfolio grid year after year, then you're not doing a very good job of strategic planning. The objective of strategic planning should not be to take the 9-block matrix as a given, but to have your efforts aimed at moving the SBUs from one category to another. What you want to see over time is more and more of your businesses moving toward the upper left corner as the result of aggressive and original strategies.

Having noted some of the ways the portfolio approach can be misleading in the development of business strategies, it is important to acknowledge that the techniques can also help to improve the quality of business strategy in two major ways. First, in many industries market share and the other variables emphasized by the techniques are indeed significant determinants of success. For SBUs competing in such industries, the portfolio approach provides useful guidelines for developing business strategy. Even when the mandates are less applicable, however, the techniques can force managers to come to terms with the realities of conditions within their markets and of their own positions within their markets. It is not necessarily true that every slowly growing industry is a poor one or that low-share businesses are doomed, but it is essential that these conditions be taken into account realistically during development of business unit plans.[1] Portfolio planning techniques help to assure that this happens and that all of the business units are not permitted to assume that sales and profits will automatically continue to grow. One indication that the techniques can benefit business unit strategies is the audit that General Electric conducted of its planning system in the mid 1970s, wherein GE's line managers indicated that they would continue to use portfolio planning techniques even if corporate headquarters dropped the requirement.

The impact of portfolio planning on business unit strategy, then, is mixed and very much depends on the purpose for which the techniques are being used and the way in which a company develops its strategies. When portfolio planning is used solely to facilitate resource allocation choices and particularly to restructure a company, it is more likely that business strategies will be defined only in terms of cash flow and market share objectives. While sometimes helpful, this approach contains the serious hazards that key aspects of the competitive environment will be overlooked and that imaginative and detailed strategies will not be developed. Similarly, when a company develops its strategies sequentially, with the formulation of business strategy being heavily influenced by the corporate strategy, the strategic mandates of portfolio planning play a major role in shaping of the business strategy. In other companies that permit business strategies to affect corporate strategy, however, the incentive is much greater for SBU management to develop unique strategies that are not constrained by a priori corporate requirements.

When portfolio planning is used to improve the quality of business plans or to improve corporate management's understanding of its businesses, the techniques are likely to provide only some broad considerations and to be supplemented by other approaches for developing business strategy. In particular, the work of Michael Porter, which calls for detailed analysis of the units' industries and competitors and which identifies a number of successful generic strategies, is much more relevant as a guide for developing business strategies than is portfolio analysis.[2] Indeed, most recent research on business strategy has de-emphasized the importance of market share and industry growth, emphasizing instead the necessity of obtaining competitive advantage via lower costs, higher quality, or competition in a unique market niche.[3]

Portfolio planning, then, is one very important input to the development of business strategy that helps to assure that certain underlying market and competitive realities are not overlooked and that the corporation's cash needs are recognized. But it should not be the only input. Equally if not more important to the development of successful business strategy is consideration of the boundaries of the market, of whether any major discontinuities are occurring or can be made to happen, and of how competitive advantage can be built and maintained. When business strategy is equated with the strategic mandates of portfolio planning, these crucial considerations may well be overlooked. Donald Melville, CEO of the Norton Company, underscored these points when he told me, "In my mind, one of the biggest dangers of the portfolio concept is if you pay attention only to a business's position on the matrix. If that is all you pay attention to, portfolio planning can be very dangerous."

All business units either generate or consume cash and either gain or lose market share. But there is an important distinction between the generation of positive or negative cash flows and higher or lower market shares as the result of strategic actions aimed at improving a unit's competitive position versus making cash flow the major objective of business strategy. In the former approach, business strategy is developed after assessment of conditions and changes in the external environment and relating of them to the SBU's competences. Only after these steps are completed is the cash flow requirement of the strategy compared with the corporation's ability to provide that cash. In the latter approach, business strategy is developed to be consistent with specific cash flow and market share objectives. While both approaches have benefits and risks, the former is more likely to produce creative business strategies that are successful over a long period of time.

PORTFOLIO PLANNING AND CORPORATE STRATEGY

A review of the companies studied reveals that portfolio planning techniques have a significant effect on corporate strategy and particularly on decisions to divest or exit businesses. For example, at many of the companies, including American Standard, CIBA-GEIGY, General Electric, Dexter, Mead, Monsanto, and Uniroyal, the introduction of portfolio planning quickly resulted in decisions to exit marginal businesses. The reasons for this direct and rather dramatic impact were noted in Chapters 4 and 6. First, the techniques have a unique ability to identify businesses whose subpar performance is rooted in such weak competitive situations that it is unlikely to be corrected by virtually any amount of management attention or access to capital. And second, portfolio planning techniques enable top managers to make divestiture decisions in a detached and analytic manner and thus to avoid the emotion-laden atmosphere that usually surrounds these decisions.[4]

As was shown in Chapter 4, the divestiture of weak divisions usually has a dramatic effect on the profitability of a diversified company. Indeed, at both Dexter and General Electric, profitability had been lagging prior to the introduction of portfolio planning and rose dramatically after its introduction and the subsequent divestitures. For example, GE's average return on equity rose from 14.8% three years prior to the introduction of portfolio planning to 17.8% three years after its introduction, while for Dexter the increase was even more dramatic: from 11.0% to 17.3%. For the 21 *Fortune* 500 companies using portfolio planning and for which data were available, the figures were 8.4% and 12.1%.[5]

The survey data also revealed that the two major resource allocation problems that companies had prior to the introduction of portfolio planning were wasting resources on continued subsidization of marginal businesses and a tendency to overinvest in low-return businesses.[6] Indeed, most of the companies studied had these problems and, as a result, found their financial positions becoming more and more constrained. The divestiture of low-return businesses, which portfolio planning encourages, is a relatively easy way to overcome these problems. Don MacKinnon of CIBA-GEIGY explained:

> *Perhaps the greatest impact of portfolio planning has been in helping us to get out of problem businesses. Before, the problem businesses kept coming in with proposals to spend money to improve their deteriorating situations. In a sense, the "squeaky wheels got all the oil." The problems with that were considerable, since they couldn't earn sufficient returns on the money that was being spent and there wasn't enough money left to spend on our healthy businesses.*

That portfolio planning techniques can have such a dramatic impact on decisions about what businesses to compete in and what businesses to exit represents a significant contribution to the corporate strategies of many large, diversified companies. In a sense, portfolio planning has legitimatized divestiture decisions. Indeed, since portfolio planning techniques were first introduced in the late 1960s and early 1970s, divestiture activity has increased dramatically. Whereas in the 1960s only 10 to 15% of all acquisitions were of divested businesses, by the mid 1970s the figure had risen to 50%.[7]

Although portfolio planning is extremely relevant to the corporate strategy problem of deciding what businesses to exit, it has little impact on the *internal* growth and business development efforts of large companies. Indeed virtually every CEO I spoke with indicated that after several years of using portfolio planning, their companies were experiencing serious problems generating enough growth and new business opportunities. As a result, once financial performance had improved, most of the companies studied had changed their use of portfolio planning techniques and supplemented them with other approaches to facilitate the pursuit of internal growth and business development rather than only increased profitability. This was most apparent at General Electric after 1976, where such devices as corporate challenges, technology assessments, internal ventures, and top management emphasis on business development were added to portfolio planning techniques to encourage internal growth. Reginald Jones commented:

> One of the things that we learned about portfolio planning is that you must add to it an explicit technology component or it just won't get addressed. Another is that portfolio planning didn't point to some of the growth opportunities that we had. There simply were opportunities to fill out business areas that we otherwise wouldn't have considered. Portfolio planning by itself is simply insufficient for filling gaps between businesses and for expanding the scope of existing businesses.

To some extent it is surprising that portfolio planning does not foster greater internal growth and business development. After all, the approach does lead to the identification of those businesses that should be funded to the fullest extent to maximize their growth. Nevertheless, in most of the companies I studied the result of several years of use of portfolio planning was the accumulation of cash that was not readily invested in ongoing businesses or new business development projects. While this does not occur at all companies, the fact that it does not is usually because of major changes in the way the techniques are used or because additional planning tools are being used to supplement the portfolio approach. For example, at the Dexter Corporation, maturing divisions were encouraged to invest in growth opportunities only because the company abandoned the traditional approach to portfolio planning and required each division to balance its use and generation of cash. Interestingly, at Memorex, where an attempt was made to apply the logic of the portfolio approach to spur on both the development and the growth of new businesses, the effort did not succeed in fostering *profitable* growth.

There are several explanations as to why portfolio planning is not conducive to internal growth and business development. One is that it merely provides a way, and conditions management, to analyze only a company's existing businesses, not new areas of opportunity. Because of this, portfolio planning is an ideal tool for determining which businesses to keep and which to divest, but it offers few insights into how to expand the scope of existing businesses. Indeed with its emphasis on market share, the techniques often lead SBU managers to define their markets as narrowly as possible, in order to maximize their market shares. While this approach can be very helpful for those units that need to concentrate efforts on market niches, its use throughout a company can lead to a constant narrowing, rather than an expansion, of the company's business base.

A final reason why portfolio planning is not conducive to internal growth and business development is its focus on market share objectives and capital requirements. In contrast, new business development requires a firm commitment to development of infrastructure in terms of human resources, marketing skills, technical capabilities, and manufacturing proficiency.[8] It is these capabilities that create internal growth opportunities. To the extent that portfolio planning distracts top managers from developing these skills and resources, it serves as an impediment to new business development.

Thus with respect to corporate strategies, we can see that portfolio planning has a significant impact in helping companies to decide which businesses in their portfolio should be kept and which should be divested. But when it comes to stimulating the growth of existing businesses or encouraging the development of new businesses, portfolio planning techniques are far less useful.

The respondents to Haspeslagh's survey, for example, indicated that, after using portfolio planning for a number of years, their greatest resource allocation problem was generating enough new growth opportunities internally. Portfolio planning, then, is much more relevant for companies with resource constraints than for those seeking new opportunities.[9]

PORTFOLIO PLANNING AND INSTITUTIONAL STRATEGY

In Chapter 2, institutional strategy was defined as the determination of the basic character and vision of a company; it is what builds a sense of purpose into an organization and creates commitment to the goals and mission of the enterprise. The data from this research suggest that not only does portfolio planning overlook institutional strategy, but a company that wants both to preserve its institutional strategy and to use portfolio planning techniques must be prepared to modify the portfolio approach to conform with its basic goals and mission.

At the Dexter Corporation, for example, the institutional strategy embodies a set of notions that the company should compete only in high-value-added specialty markets and that it should be run in a way that emphasizes fairness across the divisions and the stability of the total enterprise. That Dexter is over 200 years old underscores the time-tested wisdom of the institutional strategy. For Dexter, the feature of portfolio planning theory that was in greatest conflict with its institutional strategy was the differentiated allocation of resources to its divisions. The notion that the company should allocate a disproportionately high share of resources to some divisions ran counter to Dexter's basic character, which emphasizes fairness and the pursuit of stability for all divisions. Not surprisingly, when choosing whether to modify its institutional strategy or the application of portfolio planning, Dexter chose to modify the latter. Not only does Dexter eschew differentiated resource allocation, it explicitly promotes the pursuit of balanced portfolios by all divisions, to foster stability and fairness; and it uses portfolio planning to increase the quality of business plans rather than to determine resource allocations.

At General Electric, institutional strategy is embodied in the slogan "Progress is our most important product." This commitment to progress is reflected in GE's vast corporate research and development laboratories and in the numerous new products and patents the company continually produces. Yet GE's financial position in the early 1970s and the emphasis on divestiture that portfolio planning fostered seemed to run counter to GE's institutional strategy. Reginald Jones commented on this conflict:

> When we began closing down businesses, I was very worried that this might be interpreted by our people as a lack of commitment to develop our businesses. You can't let people think that keeping up with technology and product development is unimportant. That's why, even as we began to rid ourselves of some problem businesses, I made it a special point to emphasize to our people the significant new investments that were also being undertaken.

As a means of preserving its institutional strategy, Jones's verbal encouragement of new investments and product development was insufficient; changes in the way GE used portfolio planning techniques were also necessary. The most important of these modifications was the introduction of corporate challenges in 1977 that focused the attention of all of GE's SBUs on business development and on specific areas of market opportunity. Without these development challenges and this direction, portfolio planning usually leads to an analysis only of existing businesses and to the inevitable decisions to exit some of those businesses. With business development challenges and direction, GE legitimatized the creation of new businesses as part of its strategic planning process. By so doing, the company also acted to preserve an institutional strategy of technologic progress that dates back to the company's origins in the work of Edison, Steinmetz, and Langmuir.

The Dexter and General Electric examples point to the need for companies to modify their use of portfolio planning to be consistent with their institutional strategies.* But there are probably many more companies that do not have an institutional strategy.[10] These companies must recognize that portfolio planning is not the same thing as institutional strategy and that the approach will not provide one. Portfolio planning techniques do have relevance for certain issues of corporate and business strategy and can greatly help to clarify top management's thinking about what businesses to compete in. But the techniques do not provide a vision of what a company is trying to become and what values and goals the entire organization should embody. In their widely read book, *The Art of Japanese Management*, Pascale and Athos have observed that "great companies make meaning."[11] Portfolio planning can help tremendously to clarify resource allocation choices, but it does not help to define the character and broader purposes of an organization or "to make meaning." Joe Flannery of Uniroyal explained:

> Portfolio analysis has been very helpful to us in identifying problem businesses and in getting us to face up to divestment decisions. But there is just so much cutting that you can do. Eventually you need to determine just what it is you are trying to become and what vision you are pursuing. People need to know these things, but portfolio planning is totally silent on the issue. Just knowing what businesses you are going to be in doesn't resolve the question of what it is you are trying to achieve over the long haul.

CONCLUSION: PORTFOLIO PLANNING IN HISTORICAL PERSPECTIVE

Analysis of the impact of portfolio planning techniques on each level of strategy has proved to be a fruitful undertaking. Using a

---

*This is not meant to imply that institutional strategy should never change. When it does change, however, it is usually because of the vision of a new leader or because of major environmental change or performance problems, rather than because of the use of a new technique such as portfolio planning.

variety of data, I have shown that the greatest impact and applicability of these techniques is on corporate strategy, particularly divestiture decisions. Portfolio planning techniques can be a useful analytic device to aid the formulation of business strategy, but they can also be misleading. The techniques have little impact on an enterprise's institutional strategy and are ineffective as stimulants to internal growth and business development.

These conclusions have important implications for managers in that they suggest when portfolio planning techniques can best fit the needs of a corporation and when the techniques should be either amended or discarded. For example, when a company faces very tight financial constraints, it is most appropriate to use portfolio planning to allocate resources and not to address some of its negative organizational consequences. But when resources are more plentiful or when the objective is to increase the effectiveness of business unit planning, it makes sense for the company to modify the approach and to supplement it with additional tools and techniques.

To some extent, managers may already have begun to reach the same conclusion. The data from Haspeslagh's survey, for example, indicate that, whereas close to 90% of the companies using portfolio planning techniques arrange their businesses on a portfolio grid to gain a better understanding of the relative positions of their businesses, less than half use the grids as a basis for assigning strategies to their business units.[12]

These conclusions about the relevance of portfolio planning techniques can also help place their use and popularity in historical perspective. Although the techniques date back to the mid 1960s, they first received recognition in the early 1970s, and it was not until the mid 1970s that their use became widespread. Of course, one explanation of this is the time it takes for any new idea to be embraced by major corporations; but an equally plausible one is that it was not until the early and mid 1970s that the economic environment demanded that companies adopt the strategies that portfolio planning techniques could help direct.

For many companies, including Mead and American Standard,

the early 1970s were a period of consolidation following the excesses of the conglomerate era of the 1960s. As they entered the 1970s, these companies discovered that they had acquired more businesses than they could manage or finance. When the recession of 1970–1971 brought lower profitability and cash flow to these companies, many of them faced financial crises. Portfolio planning provided a solution to these crises by providing straightforward rationales for divesting weak divisions and for not funding others. As we have already shown, these actions can have a dramatic impact on performance and cash flow.

In the mid to late 1970s, general economic conditions provided the impetus for the widespread use of portfolio planning techniques. The three most important economic conditions during this period were slower economic growth, declining levels of profitability, and high rates of inflation.[13] In Chapter 3, we saw how rather modest declines in sales growth and profitability can dramatically reduce the cash a company has available for capital expenditures. Not only was this generally the case during the 1974–1980 period, but the high rates of inflation significantly increased the cost of new plant and equipment. The combination of reduced cash flow and more expensive investment projects left many corporate managers having to ration capital to divisions that were demanding more funds than the corporation could supply, as was the case at CIBA-GEIGY and Uniroyal.

Portfolio planning techniques offered a logical response for corporations in this situation. Rather than cut investments in all divisions by a fixed percentage, portfolio planning encouraged the divestiture and milking of businesses with weak prospects and the full funding of the stronger businesses. These corporate strategy recommendations not only are sensible but they were also ideally suited to the situation facing many companies in the last half of the 1970s.

Interestingly, in a study of a much different phenomenon— mergers and acquisitions—Salter and Weinhold drew similar conclusions about the strategies managers would be likely to follow during the 1970s:

Given the competitive, economic and political environment of the 1970s, a rational strategy by corporate managers would probably include one or more of the following business policies. The first and most obvious policy would be to improve the economic viability of their existing operations and thereby reduce the risks of and improve the cash flows generated by these operations. In addition to the normal "belt-tightening" found in every downturn, one would also expect managers to rethink their long-run commitment to existing businesses. Competitive strength and strategic potential in addition to operating profitably would become a major concern. Marginal businesses that would be tolerated in easier times would be more closely scrutinized. If corporate resources are scarce, chances are that they would only be committed to businesses "carrying their own weight." Where available resources fall short of needs, marginal or unattractive businesses may well be liquidated or divested in order to free up resources that can be more profitably used elsewhere. From the manager's personal perspective, eliminating this deadweight is also very attractive. Not only would it ease the day-to-day operating pressures he faced, but it also would allow him to increase his performance in the eyes of the suppliers of capital and therefore his access to their capital.[14]

By way of contrast, it is interesting to note that companies that were able to prosper in the 1970s were far less likely to use portfolio planning than those that experienced profit and cash flow problems. For example, Perkin-Elmer, a company renowned for its planning skills, grew at rates approaching 30% during this period.[15] Horace McDonell, Perkin-Elmer's CEO, explained:

The main reason why we haven't turned to portfolio planning in the past is that we have never been cash-scarce in the company. Because of our tremendous profitability, we have always had ample cash.

The other reason is that we are a technology-driven company. The key to our success has been to invest in many high-technology areas at the same time in order to get some big winners, rather than to ration our efforts. And in high technology, it is R&D and marketing, not capital items, that are your key investments.

Clearly there are factors other than general economic conditions and company performance that help explain the dramatic increase in the use of portfolio planning techniques. These factors include the facts that the theory underlying portfolio planning directly addresses the problems CEOs face in allocating resources and that the approach can be used and modified to serve a variety of purposes. These benefits make it reasonable to expect portfolio planning to remain an important strategic planning tool, albeit in a variety of different forms and with a number of different purposes.

To forecast the future use of portfolio planning, however, the underlying economic forces that have led to their popularity must be examined. To the extent that there will always be firms that become overextended and have insufficient financial resources, portfolio planning will remain in use to facilitate resource allocation by helping to identify and cut marginal businesses. And to the extent that our future economic environment remains unconducive to the accumulation of adequate capital for new investments, portfolio planning will remain in the mainstream of strategic planning practices. But should the economy return to the stability of the 1950s and 1960s, when growth and profitability were high and inflation was low, the use of portfolio planning for resource allocation will become less relevant, though the techniques will still have some value in providing corporate managers with an understanding of their business units and of their overall portfolio of businesses. As a result, the use of portfolio planning is unlikely to disappear entirely, but the techniques will never become a substitute for the thorough development and implementation of all three levels of strategy.

8
Summary and Implications

The research conducted for this book was guided by the following questions:

1. **Why have CEOs adopted portfolio planning techniques?** How have they used portfolio planning to help them accomplish their goals? What different uses do CEOs make of portfolio planning? What causes this variation?

2. **What issues do companies face when using the portfolio approach?** What are its positive and negative organizational consequences? What impact does it have on the processes by which strategies are formulated and implemented?

3. **What impact have portfolio planning techniques had on the strategies companies have adopted?** Which strategic decisions are most positively and negatively affected? Has portfolio planning contributed to the decline in the competitiveness of U.S. companies?

The important role diversified companies play in our economy and their widespread use of portfolio planning techniques make these questions of more than just passing interest. Yet with few exceptions the questions have not been addressed through systematic study of how organizations actually use the techniques. It was this need that motivated the investigation reported here.

Several concepts were presented in Chapters 2 and 3 to help explain the patterns in the information collected. In Chapters 4 through 7, conclusions about the use and impact of portfolio planning were developed and illustrated with reference to the companies studied, the executives interviewed, and the data bases analyzed. In the chapters that follow, detailed case studies of three companies are presented. In this chapter, the findings of the entire study are summarized and their implications discussed.

SUMMARY

The Use of Portfolio Planning

For most companies, the initial use of the portfolio approach is triggered by a decline in profitability and a cash crisis. Portfolio planning is uniquely well suited for use in these circumstances because it provides precise guidelines for allocation of capital in a way that balances cash needs and uses, and because it usually results in divestiture of businesses that continually use cash but have little prospect of earning high returns. Once profitability and cash flow improve, however, a reasonable question is, why do companies continue to follow the portfolio approach?

The answer is that CEOs have been able to use portfolio planning for a number of different purposes and that typically its use changes over time, depending on the needs of the company and the agenda of the CEO. The theory underlying portfolio planning suggests that the approach could be used to help CEOs in allocating resources to the business units. And indeed, this is one of the ways companies apply the techniques. A closer examination, however, reveals that CEOs have used portfolio planning for two quite different resource allocation purposes. One is to promote divestitures and corporate restructuring, the other to guide capital allocations within the company. Although these uses both are in the category of resource allocation, they have very different risks and emphases. In general, corporate restructuring is a much riskier use of portfolio planning techniques and focuses attention on opportunities outside, rather than within, the firm.

Another use of portfolio planning is to provide top managers with a way to understand their business units and their company's overall portfolio of businesses. While this use is not predicted by the theory underlying portfolio planning, it is quite understandable in light of the diversity and size of most large companies, since a CEO cannot possibly understand the competitive and strategic circumstances facing all of the business units. By focusing the attention of top managers on just a few variables, such as market growth and market share, portfolio planning provides them with a way to gain a rudimentary understanding of their businesses. Moreover, when all of a company's business units are displayed on a growth-share or nine-block matrix, top managers can achieve a rudimentary understanding of deficiencies and imbalances in the composition of their overall portfolio of businesses.

Yet another way CEOs use portfolio planning is to improve the quality of the business units' strategies. While portfolio planning techniques by themselves are seldom sufficient for the development of detailed business strategies, they can help to assure that the business strategies take account of the unit's market share or competitive position and of the growth or general attractiveness of the industry, and that goals are set for market share and cash flow. In this way, portfolio planning can help to overcome the lack of specificity that characterizes many strategic planning efforts. In addition, application of the techniques so as to require business units to explain the results of extensive outside analyses of their business, such as those provided in PIMS (profit impact of marketing strategies) reports, can greatly help to increase the quality of business unit strategies.

It is precisely because portfolio planning serves these multiple purposes that its use has become so widespread and is likely to continue. CEOs have adopted the portfolio approach because it enables them to address key high-priority issues. But in any company, issues and priorities change as previous problems are resolved and new opportunities and problems arise. It is largely because the portfolio approach can be adapted to changing circumstances that its use has persisted.

The use, or the combination of uses, that is made of portfolio planning techniques depends on several factors and ultimately is the choice of the CEO. In general, tight financial constraints favor the use of portfolio planning for allocation of resources. On the other hand, certain administrative considerations, such as the power and influence of division managers or a CEO who has just begun his or her tenure, favor use of the techniques either to improve the quality of business unit plans or to increase corporate management's understanding of the business units and of the overall corporate portfolio. The purpose that portfolio planning techniques will serve, however, is by no means determined by these factors; this is one of the major jobs of the CEO. The effective use of portfolio planning begins with a CEO who knows his or her own objectives, who understands the company's administrative inheritance, and who appreciates the financial constraints and strategic issues facing the company. With these as starting points, the CEO has the responsibility to choose the purpose or purposes that portfolio planning will serve.

Organizational Consequences

The use of the portfolio approach inevitably poses a number of recurring organizational issues and dilemmas. While these issues are seldom acknowledged, their effective management is essential if portfolio planning is to have a positive impact.

The first and most important of these issues is the definition of business units. Typically this task is treated as requiring only technical analyses and as preliminary to the more important tasks of categorizing the units and assigning them mandates. In contrast, one of the major conclusions of this investigation is that the definition of business units is of paramount importance, because these definitions shape the way both corporate and business unit managers perceive their markets. Moreover, the definitions are also influenced by administrative and resource allocation considerations and must be responsive to changing market, competitive, and technologic conditions. As a result, top managers must be prepared to define and redefine their business units to keep abreast of changing internal and external circumstances.

Not only does portfolio planning require that careful attention be given to business unit definitions, but its use can also lead to some unfortunate self-fulfilling prophesies. The most common of these affects mature business units. When these units are labeled cash cows, receive no new investment, and are tightly controlled, the morale and performance of the unit can deteriorate far beyond what was originally anticipated, which in turn can lead to disposition of a previously healthy (albeit mature) business unit. At the same time, unquestioned support and loose control of star businesses can eventually lead to their lower profitability. Neither of these negative outcomes is inevitable, but both need to be recognized and managed if they are to be avoided.

Underlying many of the organizational consequences of portfolio planning is the issue of how the approach is related to the processes by which strategies are developed and resources allocated, and to the CEO's management approach. Portfolio planning is perhaps best suited for chief executives who wish to manage the outcomes of these processes, because the approach enables top management, usually with the aid of staff planners, to assign both strategic mandates and resource allocations to the business units. But portfolio planning can also be used in a way that is consistent with greater lower-level involvement in the strategic processes, with less reliance on staff, and with a chief executive who prefers to manage the processes by which major decisions are made. This is accomplished by having cash flow and strategic objectives negotiated between corporate and business unit management, by not labeling the strategies of the units, by allocating resources via a two-tier process, by making line management responsible for strategy, and by a variety of other actions. But more important than any of these specific actions is the conclusion they suggest: Although the portfolio approach tends to lead to a centralization of strategic processes, it can also be managed to be consistent with other approaches for developing and implementing strategy.

While this investigation has spotlighted several problematic organizational issues that are posed by the portfolio approach, it is important to acknowledge that, even with these potential drawbacks, managers have continued to use the approach. This suggests several possible conclusions. For example, at some companies top management may have decided that the benefits of the portfolio approach—greater control of resource allocation and the disposition of weak businesses—simply outweigh its negative organizational consequences. At other companies, however, top management has developed approaches for mitigating these consequences. And many companies have found that the portfolio approach can also have important positive organizational consequences. These include clarification of top management's expectations for its divisions, legitimization of different goals for the divisions, and facilitation of the divestiture of hopelessly weak businesses without blame being placed on their managers.

The use of portfolio planning, then, does not resolve the many dilemmas that are inherent in the management of a diversified corporation. It may even create some additional issues. But when the techniques are used in a way that is consistent with a company's goals and financial and organizational circumstances, their negative consequences can be diminished and their benefits can be reaped.

Impact on Strategy

The portfolio approach to strategic planning has had its greatest impact on corporate strategy decisions, that is, on decisions affecting what businesses the company will compete in and the allocation of resources among those businesses. The reason for this is that the techniques provide a relatively simple, yet insightful, way of evaluating the adequacy of the mix of current businesses and of setting resource allocation priorities. It is in the area of divestitures, however, that the approach has had its greatest impact. By helping managers identify those businesses whose subpar performance is rooted in such a weak competitive situation that performance is highly unlikely to be corrected, the approach helps top managers make divestiture decisions in a more timely, dispassionate, and analytic manner.

While portfolio planning has proven to be extremely relevant to the corporate strategy problem of deciding what businesses to exit, it has had little impact on internal growth and business development efforts. To some extent this should not be called a shortcoming of the approach, since internal growth and business development are not even addressed by portfolio planning. It is, however, a limitation to the use of the techniques and top managers must adopt additional planning approaches to ensure that internal growth and development receive adequate attention.

When used to set business strategy, the portfolio approach has a mixed effect. By itself, the approach can be very misleading if business strategy is set solely on the basis of an SBU's position on a portfolio matrix. In general, the techniques place too much emphasis on a business's growth and market share and not enough on how it can achieve competitive advantages over its rivals. When applied cautiously and in conjunction with other techniques for analyzing the industry and the competition, however, the techniques can help managers to come to terms with the realities of conditions within their markets and their own positions within them. The important point is that cash flow and market share objectives are not substitutes for sound business strategy analysis and development, and that they should be seen as the results, rather than the purpose, of strategic actions.

It is with regard to institutional strategy that portfolio planning techniques have their least relevance. The approach does not help to define the character or broader purposes of a corporation and is not a substitute for top management leadership and vision. While the approach was probably never intended for these purposes, it must not be permitted to undermine existing institutional strategies or to inhibit the development of new ones.

Finally, it is important to try to assess the impact of portfolio planning techniques on the competitiveness of U.S. corporations. While no conclusive evidence was gathered in this research, the following perspective emerges from the data collected and the conclusions drawn. First, to the extent that portfolio planning has led to underinvestment in mature businesses and to their eventual abandonment, the approach has not served the cause of competitiveness and may well have contributed to a U.S. decline in some industries. Similarly, the extent to which the approach has led top managers to concentrate their energies on acquisitions and divestitures rather than on developing effective competitive strategies for their businesses has been a negative effect. On the other hand, the realistic assessment of market and competitive conditions that portfolio planning can help foster has led to timely rationalization of capacity in some mature industries.[1] And by leading to the disposition of hopelessly weak businesses and to the reallocation of the freed-up resources to high-potential businesses, portfolio planning can contribute to economic growth rather than to decline. The important point is that, by itself, portfolio planning is neither malign nor benign. Its impact on competitiveness depends on the purposes for which and the way in which it is used.

IMPLICATIONS FOR MANAGERS

Since the findings of this investigation have implications for top managers, division (operating) managers, and staff planners, the findings relevant to each of them are considered individually.

Top Managers

Because this study was conducted from the perspective of chief executives, it has several important implications for them. The first of these is that corporate managers need to guard against equating portfolio planning with their overall strategy and need to assure that adequate attention is paid to all three levels of strategy: business, corporate, and institutional. While the great strength of portfolio planning is the intensive analysis it provides of corporate strategy, too great a reliance on its techniques can lead to the illusion that top management's sole purpose is to buy and dispose of businesses rather than to provide long-term commitment and integrity to the company's operations. As Kenneth Andrews has observed, strategic planning has too often turned "once comprehensible institutions into a crazy quilt pattern of acquisitions now often being divested or written off."[2]

Rather than deluding themselves that it is strategic simply to buy and sell businesses, top managers need to involve themselves in the development of a business strategy to ensure that each of their operations is pursuing objectives and investing in resources that will produce long-term competitive advantages. Equally important, top managers need to dedicate themselves to defining institutional goals, values, and beliefs and to making these understood and embodied in their organizations. While such tasks may lack the glamor and excitement that acquisitions and divestitures offer, they are the foundation on which great companies are built.

Closely related to this is the implication that top managers need to understand the deficiencies of portfolio planning and to ensure that these areas are addressed via other techniques, processes, and approaches. At a minimum this means ensuring that detailed industry and competitive analyses are conducted at each business unit to supplement the general prescriptions of the portfolio approach and that adequate attention is paid to internal growth and business development opportunities. When done most effectively, it means ensuring that the portfolio approach is used in a way that is consistent with and that will lead to further clarification of the company's institutional strategy.

For this to happen, it is essential that the chief executive determine the purpose or purposes that the portfolio approach will serve and the way it will be applied in the corporation. Portfolio planning can serve a number of purposes, such as aiding corporate restructuring, aiding internal resource allocations, increasing top management's understanding of its businesses, and improving business unit plans. And because it can serve these multiple purposes, portfolio planning cannot be viewed solely as a tool for developing strategy. In a very real sense, it is also a tool for the CEO to *implement* his or her strategy and objectives for the company. What this implies, of course, is that portfolio planning (or any form of planning, for that matter) cannot be used effectively unless it is related to the broader purposes of the firm, and that it is not a substitute for—and must be preceded by—CEO leadership and goal setting.

Finally, the experiences of the companies studied all point to the crucial role of the chief executive in determining how portfolio planning is used within the organization. Portfolio planning has a number of predictable organizational consequences that cannot be ignored and that should be managed in ways that fit each particular company's objectives, its purpose in using the portfolio approach, and its administrative inheritance. Given the extent to which companies differ along each of these dimensions and the number of organizational issues posed by portfolio planning, it should not be surprising that the companies that are most successful in using the techniques do so in their own unique ways. Reginald Jones emphasized this point when I interviewed him three years after his retirement:

> *Since I retired from General Electric, I've gone on quite a few boards of directors and I've learned to appreciate just how different companies are. Their businesses are different, their organizations are different, and their managers are different. And **to do effective strategic planning they all have had to approach it in somewhat different ways.***

In many writings about portfolio planning the major conclusion drawn about the role of top management is that "because market share is so strongly related to profitability, a basic strategic issue for top management is to establish market share objectives."[3] The major implication for top managers that emerges from the current study is much different. It is that the effective use of the portfolio approach begins with a CEO who understands his or her own objectives, who understands the company's administrative inheritance, and who appreciates the financial constraints and strategic issues facing the company. By addressing these issues, rather than focusing narrowly on market share, chief executives will be best able to use portfolio planning in ways that help achieve company objectives, to adapt its use to their own organizational realities, and to supplement it with other techniques and approaches.

Division Managers

Since the portfolio approach can so easily lead to centralization of strategy development, and because its prescriptions regarding business strategy are incomplete and sometimes incorrect, division managers often feel that this approach unduly constrains their ability to manage their businesses. While at times these feelings are well founded, we would argue that portfolio planning does not necessarily have to lead to greater top-management direction of business strategy and that, whether it does or does not, division managers still have the responsibility to be actively involved in setting the business strategies for their divisions.

Thus the first implication of this study for division managers is that they should not automatically view the portfolio approach as a tool by which top management will gain greater control of business strategy. Indeed when the approach is used to increase corporate management's understanding of the business units or to improve the quality of strategic thinking at the business unit level, the result is often a greater emphasis on high-quality business strategy development at the divisional level.

Even when portfolio planning is used to facilitate the allocation of resources, it is important that division managers distinguish between a top management that assigns strategic mandates and resource commitments to the divisions and one that negotiates the mandates and commitments *with* the divisions. Only in the former case are greater constraints being placed on division managers, and here we would contend that, with their greater knowledge of their own markets and opportunities, division managers have the responsibility to disagree with their assigned mandates and to recommend changes if the situation calls for it. And whether strategic mandates and resource allocation guidelines are assigned or negotiated, division managers may still benefit from the clearer understanding of corporate management's expectations that the portfolio approach fosters.

The next implication for division managers is that the use of the portfolio approach does not relieve them of responsibility for setting creative, detailed business strategies for their divisions. Simply put, the strategic mandates of portfolio planning, as determined by the position of a business on a portfolio grid, can be misleading and are not the same as a business strategy. Whereas strategic mandates are general and abstract guidelines, a successful business strategy must be specific and precise: defining the markets the business will compete in, the products that will be sold, their performance and price characteristics, the technologies employed, the way the products will be produced and distributed, and the method of financing. It is the job of division managers to address these critical dimensions of business strategy and to develop creative approaches for gaining competitive advantage, rather than concentrating solely on market share and cash flow objectives.

It is especially important that division managers of mature businesses approach the challenge of developing business strategy in this way. This is because the portfolio approach—harvesting these businesses for cash—can so often be misleading and can so easily lead to the abandonment of the business. The best method of avoiding this is for division managers to make top management aware of the legitimate investment and growth opportunities in these businesses. Often this involves the identification of high-return high-growth segments within the mature business. In fact, by managing the mature business as a "mini-portfolio"—with investment in a few growth areas and disengagement from hopeless ones—some division managers are able to improve the position on the portfolio grid of their entire business. Another approach of managers is to uncover opportunities to compete in new ways or to invest in new technologies that will give the business competitive advantages in the traditional business. No matter what the approach, the important implication is that division managers of mature businesses have a special obligation to develop creative and detailed strategies if they are to avoid the unintended disposition of their businesses.

Overall, then, portfolio planning does not reduce the need for division managers who can formulate business strategy. Precisely because the portfolio approach leads top managers to focus on corporate strategy, and because the prescriptions for individual businesses are often misleading, adequate attention must be paid to the development of successful business strategies. Even though the extent of decentralization among companies varies considerably, division managers still have the primary responsibility to see to it that this task gets done.

Staff Planners

Staff planners can best contribute to the strategic planning process by providing the detailed and time-consuming analyses that the line (operating) organization may not otherwise undertake. Examples of such analyses include competitor assessment, technologic forecasting, and consumer research. By undertaking such analyses, staff planners can contribute valuable data and insights into the strategy development process. This contribution, however, should not be confused with the development of strategies, which is the responsibility of line managers. Portfolio planning, with its jargon and numerous nuances, is particularly susceptible to being run solely by ever-larger planning staffs. But when planners alone are concerned with strategy, the quality of strategic thinking within the line organization remains unaffected and plans are less likely to be accepted and implemented. A major

implication of this study, then, is for staff planners to view themselves as *contributors* to the ongoing development of strategy in
their enterprises, but *not* as being *responsible* for strategy.

   The next implication for staff planners is that they should
recognize that there is no one right way to do strategic planning.
Rather they must develop the ability to modify the planning
approach in response to changing objectives and external conditions. Closely related to this, planners need to pay less attention
to planning forms and documents and more to the decisions and
the key issues emanating from the plans. To some extent, this
appears to be an evolutionary process. Early in the use of portfolio
planning, every business unit must adhere to a common set of
planning forms, to ensure that each business engages in common
and detailed analyses and that a common base of information is
created. As companies gain more experience with the approach,
however, less and less is gained from the filling out of planning
forms, and it makes much more sense for the planning process to
concentrate on the key issues and decisions facing each business.
This usually results in a less visible role for staff planners, and
they must be willing to make this adjustment as strategic thinking
becomes second nature throughout the company.

   Finally, staff planners have a special responsibility to understand the weaknesses and limitations of the portfolio approach
and to develop ways to overcome them. Perhaps the most important of these is the tendency of portfolio planning to mandate
strategic objectives to business units solely on the basis of grid
position. Here it is the responsibility of staff planners to not force
these objectives on the SBUs but to work with them in analyzing
whether the mandates are appropriate. In terms of its limitations,
the most important is that the portfolio approach contributes little
to internal growth and business development. Rather than simply
turning to acquisitions, the real challenge for staff planners is to
assure that the necessary human and technical resources are developed that will enable existing businesses to identify and create
new opportunities in which the corporation can profitably invest
its resources.

PORTFOLIO PLANNING—A TOOL, NOT A SOLUTION

The chief executives of America's largest corporations face a bewildering range of problems. Responsible for the actions of thousands of employees, for the safety of numerous products, and for the impact of their factories on the environment, chief executives still face the vital economic problem of allocating resources within their companies. This task, never an easy one, is all the more difficult today because of the need to comprehend the rapidly changing competitive forces in so many diverse businesses, the tendency for all the levels in the management hierarchy to support investment proposals prepared by their divisions, and the insufficiency of most accounting information to clarify senior management's options.[4]

It was in response to these problems that portfolio planning was developed in the mid and late 1960s. By focusing the attention of senior managers on the competitive performance and strategic plans of their divisions rather than on individual investment requests, portfolio planning offered significant advantages over traditional capital budgeting procedures. Indeed for many companies, and particularly for those facing financial difficulties, portfolio planning has provided a much needed solution to resource allocation problems.

But resource allocation is only one of the strategic issues facing senior managers. By its very nature, portfolio planning deals mostly with issues of corporate strategy rather than either business or institutional strategy. Yet the chief executive needs to ensure that the organization can develop appropriate business strategies and that a basic and enduring set of concepts and beliefs guide decision making within the organization. To the extent that portfolio planning keeps senior managers from addressing either of these tasks, its effects can be most harmful. It takes more than just an investment strategy to make a great company; basic purposes to guide the investments and involved operating managers to assure that the investments realize their full potential are also necessary.[5]

Whether or not portfolio planning is used, it is the responsibility of the chief executive to take an active role in the establishment and embodiment of broad purposes and objectives for the organization. With a clear sense of purpose, chief executives are then best able to adapt a planning tool, such as the portfolio approach, to serve the objectives of the corporation. Without such a sense of purpose, chief executives too often can allow portfolio planning to direct their attention to their job as banker rather than as institutional leader, and portfolio planning can even become a distraction from this more important task.

Portfolio planning, then, is not a solution to the many problems facing senior managers, nor is it a substitute for top management leadership. It is a useful tool that can help solve a number of strategic problems. Like any tool, its inappropriate use can have potentially disastrous repercussions. But if used skillfully and with a sense of purpose, it can help foster greater objectivity in resource allocation, more realistic and varied expectations for different businesses, more specific communication about objectives, greater attention to external rather than internal performance measures, and better understanding of the company's overall portfolio of businesses.

As useful as portfolio planning can be, however, it is insufficient as a prescribed approach for managing a diversified company. One chief executive, who was an enthusiastic user of the portfolio approach, described its deficiency this way:

> The missing ingredient from all portfolio analysis is any consideration of the quality of the management running your businesses. Ironically, that is probably the single most important determinant of the success of a business and its strategy.

In other words, portfolio planning is not a substitute for creativity, insight, or leadership. Companies are not merely strategic abstractions of assets to be invested in or disposed of. Rather they are composed of real businesses competing against very real competitors, staffed by fallible human beings who need leadership to give purpose to their efforts.

Part 3

Case Studies

In the preceding eight chapters, a set of concepts and findings about the use and impact of portfolio planning was developed. The supporting data cited throughout those chapters originated from several sources: preliminary study of six companies and interviews with twenty managers, three in-depth case studies, study of six additional companies and review of other published cases, analysis of two data bases, and interviews with ten chief executive officers.

This part of the book presents the three case studies in their entirety. The purpose is to provide the reader with detailed accounts of how portfolio planning has been used in three large companies, and thus with an opportunity to test the conclusions of the previous chapters against the experiences of these companies.

Each case presents an historical review of the use and impact of portfolio planning, but each concentrates on a different aspect. The study of the Dexter Corporation seeks to explain why this strong proponent of portfolio planning has chosen to make major

153

modifications in the way it applies the techniques. The description of planning at General Electric covers a time span of almost twenty years and reports several important shifts in GE's use of portfolio planning and the relation of these shifts to the changing agendas and management approaches of GE's chief executives. In contrast to Dexter and General Electric, which modified their application of portfolio planning techniques, the Memorex Corporation was vigorously managed as a portfolio of businesses to which resources and incentives were allocated on a widely differentiated basis. The Memorex case study enables us to observe some of the organizational consequences of this approach.

Significantly, the case studies present data on how portfolio planning is actually used in practice (in contrast to the many theoretical descriptions of how it should be used). Taken together, the three studies illustrate the range of uses of portfolio planning, its impact on the levels of strategy, and its many organizational consequences. They illustrate the core findings that were further corroborated by the interviews with the ten CEOs and the other data collected for this study.

9

The Dexter Corporation

A CASE STUDY OF
UNDIFFERENTIATED
RESOURCE ALLOCATION

In Chapter 1 it was noted that one of the central features of the portfolio approach is that it enables corporate management to differentiate the allocation of resources to its business units. Indeed most descriptions of the approach suggest that resources be allocated to business units on the basis of the position of the unit on the portfolio grid.

The Dexter Corporation is an example of a firm that has aggressively implemented portfolio planning techniques but whose corporate management does *not* differentiate the allocation of resources to Dexter's five major divisions. This modification of the portfolio approach cannot be attributed to a lack of understanding of portfolio planning techniques. Worth Loomis, Dexter's President, has served as Executive Director of the Strategic Planning Institute's Board of Directors and has himself written about strategic planning.[1] Indeed it was officers of the Strategic Planning Institute who recommended that I write a case study about Dexter, because the company was so active and so committed to sophisticated planning.

This chapter explores the reasons why Dexter, a company firmly committed to portfolio planning, has chosen to implement and use the techniques in a manner that many would consider contrary to the theory of portfolio planning. We will find that Dexter uses the portfolio approach not to facilitate the allocation of resources but rather to improve the quality of strategic planning at the business unit level, and that it has modified portfolio planning to be consistent with this objective.

COMPANY BACKGROUND

The Dexter Corporation was founded in 1767 as a sawmill and subsequently became a paper producer. Today it is the oldest company whose stock is traded on the New York Stock Exchange. The company's headquarters are located in Windsor Locks, Connecticut, across the street from the site of Dexter's original sawmill.

In 1958 the company was primarily a paper producer with sales of about $3 million. David L. Coffin, a seventh-generation descendant of the founding family, assumed the presidency in that year at the age of 32. Coffin described the company at the time as "a typical family-run New England company" and had plans to expand it a great deal.

David Coffin's method of expanding the company was through acquisition. A list of Dexter's acquisitions from 1960 through 1977 appears in Table 9.1. All of these mergers and acquisitions were friendly, and in many cases Dexter had considerable involvement and lengthy discussions with a candidate prior to acquisition. In one case, discussions took place for five years before an amicable acquisition was arranged.

Although the acquired businesses were previously independent entities, not all became separate divisions of Dexter. For example, all of the smaller acquisitions listed in Table 9.1 became parts of existing Dexter divisions, and one of the larger acquisitions was subsequently divided into two separate divisions. Most

TABLE 9.1. MAJOR ACQUISITIONS OF THE DEXTER CORPORATION, 1960–1977

Company Acquired	Date	Sales in 12 Months Preceding Purchase ($000)	How Acquired	Division Incorporated Into (as of 1978)
Chemical Coating	7/1/60	1,276	Purchase	Midland
Lacquer Products	5/1/62	1,434	Purchase	Midland
Midland Industries	10/31/63	4,841	Purchase	Midland
Hysol	11/29/67	6,079	Pool	Hysol
Magna	11/30/67	1,133	Purchase	Midland
Shell Adhesives	10/1/69	2,531	Purchase	Hysol
Wornow	6/30/70	988	Pool	Hysol
Puritan	3/31/73	8,576	Purchase	Mogul
Bouvet	4/1/73	10,745	Purchase	Midland
Howe & Bainbridge	10/1/76	32,100	Purchase	C.H. Dexter
Mogul	5/9/77	66,555	Pool	Mogul Water Treatment Gibco, Invenex Life Sciences
Adhesive Engineering	6/7/77	650	Purchase	Hysol

of the companies Dexter acquired had been managed by strong entrepreneurs, who were encouraged to continue managing their businesses after the acquisition.

Dexter's Strategy

By 1977, Dexter competed in four major businesses: (1) coatings and encapsulants, (2) life science products, (3) nonwoven papers and fabrics, and (4) water treatment. Despite the seemingly large differences among these businesses, Dexter had quite an explicit strategy that can be described on the institutional, corporate, and business levels.

Dexter's corporate strategy was to compete in "specialty materials that have specialty applications." In general, Dexter's products represented a small proportion of their customers' total costs, served a specialized need, and were sold to a relatively small group of customers. Examples of products produced by Dexter divisions include the interior chemical coating for beverage cans, tea-bag paper, tissue culture material, and adhesives. Some of the characteristics of Dexter's specialty materials businesses were elaborated in the company's 1978 Long-Range Plan:

> *Most of the products produced by Dexter are classified as specialty materials, rather than commodities, because they are formulated or designed to perform a specific, vital function in the manufacturing processes of Dexter customers or in their end products. These specialty materials are not sold in the high volumes normally associated with commodity businesses.*
>
> *Dexter specialty materials require a high degree of technical service on an individual customer basis. The value of these specialty materials stems not just from their raw materials composition, but from the results and performances they achieve in actual use.*

Dexter's institutional strategy can be characterized by the words *stable, conservative, equitable, fair,* and *analytic.* A good example of Dexter's analytic approach is the statement of corporate objectives that had been developed since 1958 (Figure 9.1).

1. To develop the corporation so that it can *achieve* and maintain over the ten-year period a *10% to 15% increase in net income per share each year*. This would come from a target 12% internal growth and the balance in acquisitions and special projects.
2. To carry out the above task while:
   a. Increasing dividends as profit increases but not necessarily by as large a percentage.
   b. Not yielding management control to an outside concentrated group of stockholders.
   c. Maintaining a strong financial position by:
      (1) Achieving an overall corporate return on total capital in excess of 12.5% after taxes.
      (2) Limiting investment in nonproduction facilities to that which is necessary to the growth and maintenance of the business.
      (3) Utilizing the leverage of debt but not exceeding a debt-to-equity ratio of 40%.
3. To improve the qualitative nature of Dexter's earnings by improving:
   a. The company's participation in *recognized growth markets*.
   b. The company's dollar volume in *high-margin proprietary products*.
   c. Emphasis on marketing position.
   d. By limiting the company's dependence on a single -product/single customer market to 10% to 15% of its sales volume.
4. At the same time, to *maintain* the company's reputation for:
   a. *New product* introduction from *within*.
   b. Being a leader in its field of operation.
   c. Having a *low degree* of vulnerability to technoeconomic and governmental factors outside the corporation control.
   d. A *high level* of management expertise both at the corporate level and in divisions.
   e. Maintaining a *logical grouping* of its businesses.
   f. Maintaining a *sound financial* reputation.

   To make such acquisitions as are necessary to carry out all the aforementioned objectives provided that such acquisitions are in related fields and will not damage the company's qualitative image.

   Consistent with the above objectives, the corporation's *international* operation should represent not more than 30% of the total corporate profits either through export from the United States or growth in manufacturing overseas. The competitive nature of overseas markets requires emphasis on manufacturing abroad, in which case we prefer to own the equity, except in special situations.

Figure 9.1. Dexter Corporate Objectives Developed by Management (to 1978) (Source: Corporate Development Long Range Planning Meeting June 1970; 1st Rev., October 16, 1970; 2nd Rev., June 25, 1971 3rd Rev., February 1972; 4th Rev., May 1972; 5th Rev., June 1978.)

The objectives reflect a strong desire to maintain stable increases in earnings, to earn a high return on capital, and to not lose control of the company to an outside group. Dexter's emphasis on high returns and stability rather than on growth is at the core of the company's institutional strategy or basic character. For example, in 1978 Dexter ranked 528 on *Fortune's* list. Yet Dexter did not have an objective of reaching the top 500. When the company did make the *Fortune* 500 in 1980, I called Worth Loomis to congratulate him. He was pleased at the event but was very low-key. He explained that, other than some short-term favorable publicity, he did not think that making the 500 mattered much at all. This lack of emphasis on growth for growth's sake has a tremendous impact on the way the company is managed, as does Dexter's conservative, fair, and equitable approach to business. Conservatism, equity, and fairness run deep in this old New England company, as was evident during the 1960s, when the company was making acquisitions. Even in the heyday of the conglomerate era, Dexter eschewed that label and used conservative accounting methods to record its acquisitions.

Dexter's business strategies were less clearly defined than either its corporate or institutional strategies and were developed at the level of the strategic business segment.* Two common characteristics of Dexter's business strategies, however, were that they were supposed to result in strong competitive positions and in profitable performance. Worth Loomis pointed out that being a major competitor in each of its markets was very important to Dexter:

> For strategic planning purposes Dexter is divided into twenty-six
> Strategic Business Segments. . . . In twenty-two of these twenty-six
> units, we are number one or number two in market share. Sales in

---

*Strategic business segments (SBS) is the term Dexter used to designate its business. These SBSs are roughly equivalent to strategic business units. Due to the specialized nature of Dexter's products and markets, however, Dexter's strategic business segments tend to be smaller than typical strategic business units.

1977 to markets in which we are number one or number two totaled over 70 percent of our expected sales. Fundamentally, we regard this characteristic as our major strength.

The emphasis on profitability stemmed from Dexter's corporate objective to achieve a pre-tax return of at least 25% on total capital. For Dexter's divisions, which usually comprised four to six business segments each, there were strong incentives to earn a pretax return on investment of 35%.

Organization and Management

Dexter was organized into five operating divisions. These divisions roughly coincided with Dexter's largest acquisitions and were the primary operating units in the company. Budgets, performance monitoring, and incentive compensation were all tied to a division's total activities. For major strategic and operating decisions, it was the division president who almost always met and interacted with senior corporate management.

Dexter prided itself on the decentralized manner in which it approached dealings with its divisions, and on the fact that Dexter's corporate headquarters staff in 1978 totaled only 19 people, including secretarial staff, assuring that there would be only minimal corporate meddling in divisional affairs. The Management Committee, which met once a month to review results and plans, included four corporate officers and the five division presidents. Worth Loomis cited three advantages of decentralization:

(1) Decentralization naturally keeps corporate overhead to a minimum. . . . (2) It makes life a hell of a lot more interesting for people in the divisions because it allows them to run their own shows. (3) We think it produces better decisions because they are closer to the source of fact, particularly the marketplace.

Dexter's small corporate staff and the autonomy granted the divisions meant that one of the ongoing administrative considerations of corporate management was the opinions and perceptions of the division presidents. Some of these division presidents were the former owners of their business and held a good deal of stock in Dexter. Thus their sensibilities were of considerable importance.

Two examples of the power and emphasis on divisions are Dexter's approaches to management development and incentive compensation. Even though the corporate office reviewed second-level division personnel annually, the selection and training of division personnel at all levels was the province of the division president. Even in the case of the position of division president, the outgoing president's recommendation for his replacement was sought and generally followed.

Incentive compensation was closely related to divisional performance. The bonus pool for the entire division increased as divisional return on net assets went from 15% to 35%. Although Dexter had a philosophy of profit sharing for all employees and the disbursements of each division's bonus pool were submitted to the corporate office, it was the division presidents who determined the criteria for distributing the pool to division personnel.

As Dexter's president, Worth Loomis had a management approach that was quite compatible with Dexter's decentralized philosophy. Loomis, who was 53 years old in 1978, had joined Dexter in 1970 as vice president of finance after a career in manufacturing. In 1975 he became president of Dexter. Loomis was a thoroughly professional manager, well versed in the latest business theory and eager to learn of new approaches that could benefit Dexter. Though he closely monitored divisional performance and had introduced more and more sophisticated planning techniques, Loomis also strongly believed in the importance of maintaining strong divisional control of strategy. He commented:

> I like to run the company so that we have five strong divisions with division presidents who can make big decisions, rather than having all the big decisions made at the corporate office.

In terms of the concepts developed in Chapter 3, Loomis managed the processes by which strategies were formed and also paid close attention to administrative constraints (such as the power and importance of the division managers). In terms of his agenda, the major items in 1978 were to see that Dexter's strong profit performance continued, that planning concepts were used throughout the company, and that management concepts such as product managers, business teams, and task forces were encouraged as much as possible.

THE INTRODUCTION OF PORTFOLIO PLANNING

Since the late 1950s, Dexter had prepared five-year sales and profit plans. This form of long-range planning was found inadequate during a capital shortage in the early 1970s. As shown in Table 9.2, between 1968 and 1973 Dexter's long-term debt mushroomed from $5.1 million to $12.7 million, and working capital requirements increased nearly fourfold, from $5.8 million to $19 million. While Dexter's capital requirements were accelerating, profits grew rather slowly, from $2.6 million in 1968 to $5.3 million in 1973. In 1973, the Boston Consulting Group (BCG) was retained to help top management deal with this capital shortage.

Although the consulting study concluded that Dexter's investment policy had been "reasonably consistent with the portfolio management approach," the study served as a catalyst for efforts to identify which of Dexter's businesses should be supported and which divested. Indeed between 1973 and 1977, a number of slowly growing and weaker performing businesses were divested or liquidated. But even though Dexter displayed its portfolio on various growth/share matrices, it made no attempt to assign each business an explicit category such as dog, cow, or star. One reason was that each of Dexter's divisions tended to have a balanced portfolio. Another reason was that each business was part of a division, and corporate management wanted to avoid labeling a portion of a division manager's responsibility. A final reason given by Dexter managers for this modification to the portfolio approach was that, by not labeling business strategies, the com-

TABLE 9.2.   FINANCIAL PERFORMANCE OF THE DEXTER
CORPORATION, 1968–1973

Item	Performance ($ Million[a])					
	1973	1972	1971	1970	1969	1968
Net sales	$100.2	$66.2	$53.7	$54.2	$50.7	$42.6
Cost of sales	63.5	42.5	33.4	33.7	30.9	26.3
Marketing and administration	17.1	9.6	8.3	8.0	7.4	6.2
Research and development	5.1	4.0	3.6	3.5	3.1	2.4
Income before taxes	10.7	8.1	6.7	6.8	7.0	5.5
Net income after taxes	5.3	4.0	3.3	3.4	3.3	2.6
Working capital	19.0	16.2	15.4	14.7	8.3	5.8
Long-term debt	12.7	5.7	3.8	4.2	4.7	5.1
Total assets	87.6	64.0	54.6	51.1	46.0	36.0
Earnings on average shareholder's equity	11.0	9.2	8.1	9.0	12.9	11.9
Net income per share (dollars)	$ 1.28	$ .98	$ .81	$ .84	$ .90	$ .70

[a]Except net income per share, in dollars.

pany was able to avoid "the motivational and political problems
of harvesting a whole division" and could instead concentrate on
improving the quality of strategic thinking within each division.

Defining Strategic Business Segments

Another very important result of the Boston Consulting Group
study was that it aroused both corporate and divisional interest in
business-by-business approaches to planning. Prior to this, long-
range plans had been prepared only on a divisional basis. In 1973,
BCG had identified 16 of Dexter's businesses that were to be used
as the basis for planning. But because these businesses did not

necessarily coincide with how Dexter was organized, it was difficult to get much support for planning their future. Bob Ottman,
Dexter's manager of corporate development, explained:

> We had gotten into some traps with the BCG-defined business
> segments. They weren't traps that we understood at the time, but as
> we went along people became less and less interested because the
> segments were meaningless to them.

The response to this problem was designation of a new set of
strategic business segments that would be the basis for Dexter's
strategic planning. These segments were designated in 1977, about
six months before we began our research at Dexter. Table 9.3 lists
Dexter's 26 strategic business segments. Interestingly, all of the
segments were parts of existing Dexter divisions, and none of the
segments crossed divisional boundaries. Bob Ottman described
how the segments were chosen:

> One of the things Worth Loomis and the corporate development
> department decided upon when we were going to pick these seg-
> ments was that we wanted no more than thirty business segments
> for the whole corporation—no more than five or six per division;
> otherwise we'd have just too many things to worry about. Next, we
> wanted the segments we picked to be something people could
> associate with, segments that people could identify and were fami-
> liar with. We wanted more background to avoid some of the traps
> we'd gotten into with BCG-defined segments.

> Some of the divisions contend that we didn't let them get involved
> in the definition of the segments, but in fact it was, and is, an
> interactive process. The Midland Division, for instance, is unsatis-
> fied with the ones we picked, so they're coming in in a few weeks
> and we're going to sit down and discuss what they think would be
> appropriate. I laid out the guidelines: give me something that is
> firm and rich enough so that I can write a description about it,
> define distinct competitors, come up with a market share on it, and
> put a growth rate on it.

Dexter's experiences in designating strategic business segments illustrates the need to consider administrative and techni-

TABLE 9.3. STRATEGIC BUSINESS SEGMENTS (SBSs)
OF THE DEXTER CORPORATION, 1977

Division	Business Name	SBS Number
C. H. Dexter	Tea Bag (paper)	1
	Fibrous Casing	2
	Medical Disposables—nonwovens	3
	Vacuum Bag (paper)	4
	Sailcloth & Hardware	5
	Recreational Fabric	6
Gibco, Invenex	Tissue Culture	7
	Diagnostics	8
	Lab Animals	9
	Medos	10
	International	11
	Invenex	12
	Heun/Norwood	13
Mogul	Water Treatment	14
	Puritan (sanitation chemicals)	15
Hysol	Molding Powder	16
	Coating Powder	17
	Liquid Coatings	18
	Wornow	19
	Adhesives	20
Midland	Packaging (coatings)	21
	Building—prefab (coatings)	22
	Recreational (coatings)	23
	Nonstick (coatings)	24
	Wood-Bouvet	25
	Other Midland	26

cal factors when making these choices. When the Boston Consulting Group first defined Dexter's business units in 1973, the only consideration was technical—that each business unit correspond to unique markets or industries. This procedure was found lacking when "people became less and less interested because the segments were meaningless to them."

Defining business units that are meaningful in the sense that people in the organization relate to them was one administrative consideration that shaped the designation of strategic business units at Dexter. Another was the power and influence of the division presidents, who were encouraged to participate in the process of defining the units. Finally, Worth Loomis' time constraints also played a role in determining the definitions of the business segments. At Dexter, with its specialty materials product line, it is possible to identify numerous candidates for SBU designation. Nonetheless, Dexter limited the selection to no more than 30 because this was consistent with Loomis' management approach, which favored managing the process by which the divisions developed their strategies rather than determining the substance of each division's strategy.

Dexter's choice of business units, of course, also reflects the technical consideration of trying to define business units that correspond to distinct markets. But the important point is that this factor alone does not explain either the shortcomings of the original designations or the newly defined business segments. To explain these events requires a conceptual scheme that also includes administrative considerations and the management approach of the CEO.

PORTFOLIO PLANNING IN 1978

By 1978, after five years of experience with portfolio planning, Dexter's financial results had improved dramatically. As shown in Table 9.4, between 1973 and 1977 sales had grown at over 22% per annum, while net income had grown at almost 25% and return on equity increased from 12 to 18%. By 1978, Dexter was producing enough cash internally to fund all of its investment projects and was actually reducing the percentage of debt in its capital structure.

Dexter's planning in 1978 was done by the strategic business

TABLE 9.4. FINANCIAL PERFORMANCE
OF THE DEXTER CORPORATION, 1973–1977

Item	Performance ($ Million[a])				
	1977	1976	1975	1974	1973
Operating Results					
Net sales	$315.8	$255.1	$204.9	$199.7	$140.7
Cost of sales	198.4	158.6	126.3	128.4	83.5
Marketing and administration	61.0	50.4	42.9	39.4	31.7
Research and development	9.8	8.0	6.6	6.1	5.3
Income before interest, depreciation, and foreign exchange	41.4	34.6	25.1	22.2	17.0
Net income (after interest, depreciation, and taxes)	18.6	15.4	10.3	9.2[b]	7.6
Working capital	61.2	53.4	44.1	40.9	28.3
Total assets	185.5	176.9	146.8	149.3	113.3
Other Data					
Debt to capital	16.0%	19.8%	21.5%	25.9%	19.7%
Return on average stockholders' equity	18.3%	17.3%	13.2%	13.0%	12.0%
Net income per share (dollars)	$ 2.04	$ 1.70	$ 1.15	$ 1.01	$ 0.85
Dividend payout	29.4%	23.9%	22.1%	22.4%	20.9%
Price-earnings range	$ 10–7	$ 10–5	$ 9–5	$ 11–5	$ 18–8

[a]Except net income per share and price-earnings range, in dollars.
[b]Reduced by $3.3 by a change in accounting from first-in first-out (FIFO) to last-in first-out (LIFO).

segments. Each SBS was required to prepare a five-year plan, to articulate a long-term competitive strategy, and to present various analyses of its business. Some of the information reported in these long-range plans was: historical and projected five-year sales growth; next year's budgeted sales (in dollars and units); current, budgeted, and five-year planned gross and net profit margins; and planned capital expenditures over the next five years. In addition, each SBS prepared a fact sheet that defined the served market, identified the competitors, and quantified the market's size and the market shares of each competitor. Figure 9.2 is the fact sheet that was prepared in 1978 by SBS number 16, Molding Powder, which was part of the Hysol Division. One interesting aspect of the fact sheet is that the $39 million molding-powder market was divided into two market segments: general purpose and semi-conductor. That each of these market segments was not considered a separate SBS reflects the facts that only a limited number of

---

Definition of served market: Epoxy molding powder for encapsulation of electrical and electronic devices on a worldwide basis.

Competitive structure: (market share):

General Purpose		Semiconductor	
Hysol	44%	Hysol	15%
Competitor A	15	Competitor A	49
Competitor C	20	Competitor B	14
Others	21	Others	22
	100%		100%

Hysol sales in 1977: $3.1 million + $ 4.7 million= $ 7.8 million

Size of total market: $7.0 million + $32.0 million= $39.0 million

$$\text{Percent of total served market} \quad \frac{7.8}{39.0} = 20\%$$

Projected real growth: 11%

Figure 9.2.   Fact Sheet of Molding Powder, Strategic Business Segment Number 16, Hysol Division

SBSs could be reviewed by the CEO and that Dexter competed in very specialized, and thus narrowly defined, market segments.

Each SBS was required to analyze its business using a variety of portfolio planning techniques. For example, Dexter made extensive use of the PIMS model as one way of quantifying and comparing the performance of the SBSs. Mr. Loomis thought it was particularly important for each SBS to present its plans in a variety of ways, using a range of analytic techniques. This prevented the rigid application of one approach and, it was hoped, assured that all important issues were considered.

The long-range plans of each division's SBSs were compiled in the long-range planning manual. The long-range planning meeting, a three-day event held each June, was attended by the five division presidents, the corporate officers, and some key divisional and corporate staff employees. Typically 15 to 20 people attended. At the meeting, the plans of each SBS were presented and critiqued. Issues affecting all of the SBSs, such as investment criteria, were also discussed. In addition, the question of which businesses were likely divestment candidates was reviewed.

Dexter had standard capital appropriation procedures that did not explicitly link capital investments to the strategy of the SBS. For example, all investments were evaluated on a discounted cash flow basis and were required to exceed the 15% hurdle rate. This hurdle rate was applied to all SBSs, regardless of their strategy, as Loomis did not feel that portfolio planning mitigated the need for discounted cash flow analysis.

In a very basic modification to the theory underlying the portfolio approach, Dexter did not attempt to differentiate the allocation of resources to its five divisions. Although certain SBSs within each division were cash generators and others were cash users, each Dexter division was required to maintain a balanced portfolio of its strategic business segments. Thus there was minimal flow of capital among Dexter's five divisions. Loomis explained the reasons for this practice:

> We have not often faced the hard issues of funding some businesses and not others. When we have, we said that each division

must be a "tub standing on its own bottom." Of course, we have applied some "English" to be sure that no high-potential businesses were shortchanged.

Since every division has had both cash-generating capability and growth opportunities, there has been no real need to move a lot of funds from one division to another. But even if this were not the case, we would be hesitant to do so because of the motivational and political problems of harvesting a whole division.

By not having cash flow between divisions, Dexter has chosen to create five balanced divisional portfolios of businesses rather than one balanced corporate portfolio. This approach stands in sharp contrast to the theory underlying portfolio planning and seemingly eschews some of the major benefits to be gained from the techniques. Yet as we noted earlier, Dexter and Worth Loomis are quite serious about these techniques and are convinced that this modification makes sense for them.

Since Dexter was obviously not using the portfolio approach to facilitate resource allocation, what purpose did the continued use of the approach serve? The answer is that the techniques were used to improve the quality of strategic thinking and planning at the divisional and business segment level. Worth Loomis described this use of portfolio planning:

Portfolio planning tools, such as PIMS and the growth-share matrix, confront division management with information that forces them to think strategically. Without this information, division managers tend to think only about their own business. The portfolio tools force them to think about their business in relation to the marketplace and in relation to the other opportunities the company has.

The important thing about our planning forms, such as the PIMS input forms, is that they force our divisions to confront certain information and the conclusions of certain analyses. I guess I still believe strongly in decentralization and that decisions and insights about how to compete should come from those people closest to the marketplace.

The reasons why Dexter used the portfolio approach in this way can best be explained in terms of the forces shaping strategic

TABLE 9.5. FORCES SHAPING STRATEGY FORMULATION AND IMPLEMENTATION
IN THE DEXTER CORPORATION

Portfolio and Strategic Analysis

Differentitate resource allocation
between divisions

Administrative Considerations

Divisions very autonomous
Divisions powerful
Divisions performing well
Divisions recently independent
and many former owners still
run them
Harvesting whole divisions
creates motivational and
political problems

*Formulation and Implementation
of Strategy*

Balanced portfolios
Divisional profitability standards
Institutional strategy of stability
and fairness

Agenda and Strategic Mode of CEO

Agenda to get planning concepts
used throughout company
Preference to manage processes
rather than substance

Financial Resources Position

All divisions have cash-generating
capability and growth potential
Company strong financially

decision making. As shown in Table 9.5, with the exception of portfolio theory, the other forces indicate that Dexter should not differentiate resource allocation. Most salient of these are the administrative considerations involved in harvesting entire divisions. As discussed earlier, Dexter's divisions are quite autonomous and in many cases are run by their former owners, and Dexter encourages these entrepreneurs to continue managing their business. Treating these divisions differently is bound to pose administrative problems for Worth Loomis. Nonetheless, high on Loomis's agenda is to have portfolio planning techniques, strategic thinking, and organization concepts such as product managers and business teams, used throughout the company. Given the entrepreneurial nature of the division managers, Loomis is more concerned with getting each division to analyze its businesses in a sophisticated manner than with getting involved in disputes over which divisions will get a larger share of the capital budget.

Finally, Dexter's financial resource position indicates no pressing need to ration capital among divisions. The company is in very strong financial condition with a healthy cash flow. And the fact that Dexter's divisions have tended to have cash-generating capability and growth potential brings into question whether Dexter even has the need to differentiate resource allocation. When the weight of all of these factors is considered along with Dexter's institutional strategy of emphasizing stability and fairness, Dexter's choices to have each division maintain a balanced portfolio of businesses and to use the portfolio approach to improve the quality of business unit planning seem most reasonable.

Having each division maintain a balanced portfolio of businesses, however, does not mean that resources do not get allocated differentially within a division. It only means that funds usually do not flow between divisions. Within the divisions, however, the SBSs do receive different allocations of capital. For example, one of Dexter's divisions is made up of five strategic business segments of which one is a large supplier of cash, one is a large user of cash, and the other three come close to balancing the use and generation of cash. Another division that was beginning to generate a lot of cash from its existing business segments acquired a rapidly growing related business. This acquisition became a strategic business segment within the division and used much of the excess cash that was being generated within the division. These examples indicate that Dexter has followed a two-tier approach to resource allocation, wherein the divisions allocate a considerable portion of their resources directly to the business segments.

An interesting analogy can be made between Dexter's two-tier approach to allocation of resources within five balanced portfolios of businesses and a poker tournament. Imagine a poker tournament in which there are 25 low-stakes tables and 5 high-stakes tables. Each team has one player at each table. The high-stakes tables (divisions) can play only with the winnings provided to them from their teammates at the low-stakes tables (SBUs).

Team A organizes its efforts so that each high- stakes table can use only the winnings from 5 low-stakes tables. In other words, 5 groups of 5 low-stakes players report directly to a high-stakes player.

Team B assigns a president to distribute the winnings of the 25 small-stakes tables to the 5 high-stakes tables.

Analysis of these two approaches highlights the reasons for Dexter's two-tier approach to implementing portfolio planning. Team B's approach has the advantage of being able to place all of its resources behind a really good hand at a high-stakes table. However, the administrative problem is: How can the president gain enough time and knowledge to assess the prospects of all 25 low-stakes games, and all 5 high-stakes games, and then make meaningful comparisons among the games and transfer funds among them? Multiplying the number of poker tables, information, and uncertainty, by a factor of 10 probably creates a closer approximation of the problem facing the presidents of most large diversified companies.* Of course, Team A's approach, which is the one followed by Worth Loomis at Dexter, has the weakness of

---

*The factor of 10 reflects only the greater size of most diversified companies. It does not begin to account for the fact that much more information is required to understand a business than a hand of poker.

possibly having to fold while it is holding a good hand at one of the high-stakes tables. But the small size of Dexter's corporate staff makes it difficult for Loomis to analyze all of Dexter's businesses, and his management approach is to have his division presidents (high-stakes players) pay close attention to their five strategic business segments (low-stakes players) and decide which business segments should produce or consume cash.

When I explained this analogy to Mr. Loomis after I finished my research at Dexter, he was very enthusiastic about it and even used it himself to explain to others the way that portfolio planning was used at Dexter.

THE HYSOL DIVISION

To gain a better understanding of how Dexter's portfolio planning practices influence the way strategies are formulated and implemented at Dexter, I studied the molding powder business segment of Dexter's Hysol Division in greater detail. I chose the Hysol Division because it was planning for increased growth over the next five years, yet the performance of its molding powder business segment had been disappointing. My study of this business revealed the depth of commitment of Dexter's top management to its way of using and modifying the portfolio approach.

The molding powder business was one of five strategic business segments within the Hysol Division. During the 1972–1977 period, it experienced real annual compounded growth of 17%, and similar sales gains were expected for the next five years. The molding powder business segment had been further divided into two subsegments—electrical and semiconductor grades. Semiconductor molding powders were used to make the plastic-like material that encapsulates integrated circuits, and Hysol was the second largest supplier of the powders (Figure 9.2). The semiconductor subsegment had been growing in excess of 25% per year and accounted for the largest portion of this SBS's sales. This trend was expected to continue.

Electrical molding powders were sold to firms like General Electric and Westinghouse and were used to encapsulate bushings, transformers, and other conventional electrical components. This business was growing by between 5% and 10% per year, and Hysol was the largest supplier of these products (Figure 9.2).

When semiconductor manufacturers first started to use molding powders as encapsulants, Hysol, because of its experience in electrical-grade molding powders, had a major position. Until the early 1970s the semiconductor industry was quite fragmented, and Hysol concentrated on serving the needs of the numerous smaller integrated circuit (IC) manufacturers rather than the few large firms. Hysol's emphasis on low-volume but high-margin molding powders gave the division the strong reputation as "the drugstore of the industry." During the 1970–1971 recession, however, most of the small manufacturers folded, and four or five major manufacturers of ICs emerged.

In 1974, the molding powder business was the subject of a Boston Consulting Group study.* This study, motivated by a desire to understand the business better, had resulted in a clearer idea of the differences between the electrical and semiconductor molding powder segments. With regard to the latter it was observed that:

1. Semiconductor molding powder was the high-growth segment of the molding powder business (20+% through 1978).

2. Although Hysol was the largest manufacturer of molding powder, it was number 2 in the domestic semiconductor subsegment (but number 1 outside the United States) and had been losing share.

3. The battle for a viable long-term position in epoxy molding powders would be won or lost in the United States semiconductor segment.

4. A standard semiconductor molding powder would emerge

*This was the first Boston Consulting Group study done on an individual business at Dexter.

during the next two to three years, after which market gains would be difficult.

Although the report had accurately predicted the growth of the market, it had incorrectly assumed that a standard semiconductor molding powder would evolve quickly. In fact, the development of new semiconductor technologies and applications, and the importance of improved molding powders to existing applications, had made new product developments important to continued product acceptance.

That BCG was incorrect in assuming that a standard semiconductor molding powder would emerge is illustrative of the problems that can arise when portfolio planning techniques are applied to questions of business unit strategy. The experience curve is based on the assumption that market share is important because products are susceptible to cost reductions. The application of portfolio planning concepts to semiconductor molding powders leads to a business strategy of developing a standard product and very specialized manufacturing equipment in order to lower the cost of the product. In the case of semiconductor molding powders, a more detailed analysis of the industry suggests a business unit strategy of heavy and continued investment in research and development and a flexible approach to manufacturing.

As a result of Hysol's own thinking and the BCG report, it was decided that the division should attempt to improve its market share position in semiconductor molding powders. Actions included increasing and focusing research and development, seeking closer relationships with major customers, and separating electrical- from electronic-grade molding powder. The original objective of the division had been to equal the size of its largest competitor by 1981–1982. By 1977, however, market share had not increased and was still one-third that of Hysol's largest competitor. While the division had scaled back some of its earlier objectives, the 1978 plans for the semiconductor molding powder business and PIMS analyses of the business forecast market share to increase from 15% in 1977 to 33% by 1982.

Despite the positive forecasts for the semiconductor molding powder business, the business was still the subject of considerable concern within Dexter. The business had been one of the most studied in the company and, though market share was stabilizing, no improvements had been made. Three reasons were commonly cited to explain this lack of progress. The first was that Hysol had made major strategic blunders by not recognizing the growth of the molding powder segment and by pursuing its "drugstore of the industry" strategy. Following the BCG's recommendation to pursue a standard product was another strategic error. Thus the poor performance of semiconductor molding powder could be seen as the price paid for the missing of major market changes.

A second explanation was the problems were organizational in origin. Specifically, the growth of the semiconductor molding powder market had coincided with the management transition from the entrepreneur who had sold Dexter the Hysol Division to a professional manager. Prior to this transition, the division had probably become conservative in its investments and R&D. Moreover, Hysol's sales force was organized to sell to different industries rather than to promote the use and development of products such as semiconductor molding powders. When the new general manager took over in 1973, he immediately segmented the sales force by product groupings and appointed product sales managers.

The third explanation of the problems with semiconductor molding powders was that Dexter's approach to portfolio planning, requiring each division to maintain a balanced portfolio of businesses, had discouraged the Hysol Division from making the necessary investments in the semiconductor molding powder business. The problem was particularly noticeable in the Hysol Division because other strategic business segments were also growing rapidly and requiring cash investments. The Hysol Division president discussed this argument in detail:

> I would say going back one, two, or three years ago, that due to the constraints of the profit sharing and the incentive program for the divisions, we probably underinvested in our two growth businesses—semiconductor molding powder and adhesives—in order

to keep a balanced portfolio within the division. Today only because we're on a high-growth year, we are generating enough funds internally so that we can fund adhesives to the proper level. We are still underfunding semiconductors—not intentionally, but we don't have the technical staff we need, and that is a definite effect of not making the investment in the people two to three years ago.

Dexter corporate says we (the division) should have our own balanced portfolio of businesses. Currently, we are supposed to have a net positive cash flow and a divisional pretax ROI of 35 percent. BCG says that, if we have the opportunity, we should be able to use cash generated from other Dexter businesses to grow some of our high-opportunity businesses. I think there is some reluctance in accepting the fact that Hysol as a division can grow product lines at a greater rate than 20 percent.

Although these comments reveal a concern with the way Dexter used portfolio planning techniques, corporate management did not change its approach to portfolio planning because of the situation with the semiconductor molding powder business. The reasons for this have to do with Dexter's institutional strategy, with Worth Loomis' approach to his job, and with administrative considerations. Dexter's institutional strategy values conservatism and fairness. Diverting excess funds to semiconductor molding powder, in light of its past performance, was neither conservative nor fair. As Worth Loomis commented, "It is not clear to me that Hysol's semiconductor molding powder business will be so successful in the future that it justifies our diverting still more cash to fund that business."

Having Worth Loomis divert cash to semiconductor molding powders also runs counter to his approach of managing the processes that produce strategic outcomes. Although the situation facing the semiconductor molding powder business was an important one to Dexter and particularly to the Hysol Division, the business still represented only 1.5% of Dexter's total sales. For Loomis to get so involved with the substance of such a small business segment as to divert funds to it is simply inconsistent with his management approach. Finally, not requiring the Hysol

Division to maintain a balanced portfolio would raise two immediate administrative problems. First, other divisions would also want relief from the requirement. And second, Dexter's corporate management, with its very small corporate staff, would soon find itself making resource allocation decisions about which they lacked substantive knowledge and experience.

For these reasons, and because there were other explanations for the poor performance of the semiconductor molding powder business, Dexter did not alter its approach to portfolio planning. Instead corporate management has maintained the modifications to the portfolio approach because these modifications are consistent with the company's healthy financial resource position, with the company's administrative inheritance, with Worth Loomis' management approach, and with the company's purpose in using the approach.

10

The General Electric Company

A CASE STUDY OF CHANGING APPROACHES TO PORTFOLIO PLANNING

No company in the United States has received more recognition for its management skill and planning acumen than the General Electric Company. In a 1981 poll of the chief executive officers of the *Fortune 500* companies, Reginald Jones, GE's CEO until April 1, 1981, was chosen as the best CEO, and General Electric was voted the first choice as the company "with the best overall management."[1] GE's approach to strategic planning has also been recognized as the most sophisticated in U.S. industry. Dan Fink, who had become the senior vice president for corporate planning and development in 1979, commented:

Shortly after I took this job, I visited some people at the Defense Department because I had heard that they had just finished an exhaustive survey of industrial planning systems. They told me I was probably inheriting the world's most effective strategic planning system and that Number Two was pretty far behind.

With such acclaim for its planning skills, it is not surprising that there have been numerous published descriptions of GE's approach to strategic planning.[2] Some of these descriptions have been prepared by planners on GE's staff, others by journalists, and some by researchers. In addition, many managers from U.S. and foreign companies have been given a "one-day tour" of GE's planning system. This usually consists of having conversations with three or four members of the planning staff and receiving a thick packet of brochures and speeches that describe how General Electric plans.

I, too, have had the one-day tour and have read the packet of speeches and articles. But my study of General Electric's planning extended beyond this for another 13 months, during which I was able to interview numerous line managers within the General Electric Company and to track the progress of three new business ventures and the planning of a major new strategic program. In addition, I interviewed both Reginald Jones and his successor, Jack Welch, and discussed with them their views of GE's planning system and their assessments of its impact.

When I began my research at General Electric, I expected to find a very orthodox implementation of industry attractiveness/business position portfolio tools and a heavy reliance on PIMS (profit impact of marketing strategy), which had its genesis as an internal General Electric study. When the very first manager I interviewed told me that GE had not seriously used PIMS in several years, I knew that my initial hypothesis was going to be revised.

During the course of my research, I realized that GE's approach to portfolio planning had changed several times during the 1970s and was changing again in the 1980s. These modifications to the portfolio approach were largely the result of changes in the agendas and management approaches of GE's chief executive officers. The description that follows not only chronicles the development of strategic planning at General Electric but also seeks to uncover some of the underlying reasons for the adjustments the company has made in the way it plans.

ORIGINS OF STRATEGIC PLANNING AT GENERAL ELECTRIC

As the decade of the 1960s was nearing a close, the financial resources of the General Electric Company were becoming increasingly constrained. As explained in Chapter 3, this does not mean that General Electric was near bankruptcy or even operating at a loss. As shown in Table 10.1, GE earned nearly $330 million in 1970. But this level of profits was no higher than had been achieved in 1965, even though sales had increased 40%. And this profitless growth came at the same time that three major ventures—commercial jet engines, mainframe computers, and nuclear power plants—were demanding more and more of the company's financial resources. Pressure on corporate management was mounting: GE's "sacred Triple A bond rating" was in jeopardy. It was in response to these financial constraints that General Electric began to look for new forms of strategic planning.

Improving GE's financial situation and developing new planning approaches were not easy tasks. In 1968, GE was widely diversified and was decentralized into 10 groups, 46 divisions, and over 190 departments.* Indeed diversification and decentralization had been the major strategic and organizational thrusts of GE's two most recent CEOs, Ralph Cordiner (1950–1963) and Fred Borch (who succeeded Cordiner and was still CEO in 1970). Under decentralization, the departments became the organizational building blocks of General Electric, each with its own product/market scope and its own marketing, finance, engineering, manufacturing, and employee relations functions. One GE executive noted:

> In the 1950s, Cordiner led a massive decentralization of the company. This was absolutely necessary. GE had been highly central-

---

*As a measure of diversification, GE competed in 23 of the 26 two-digit SIC industry categories.

TABLE 10.1. STATISTICAL SUMMARY FOR THE GENERAL ELECTRIC COMPANY, 1960–1970

Item[a]	1970	1969	1968	1967	1966	Year 1965	1964	1963	1962	1961	1960
Sales of products and services	$8,726.7	$8,448.0	$8,381.6	$7,741.2	$7,177.3	$6,213.6	$5,319.2	$5,177.0	$4,986.1	$4,666.6	$4,383.2
Net earnings	328.5	278.0	357.1	361.4	338.9	355.1	219.6	272.2	256.5	238.4	218.7
Earnings per common share	3.63	3.07	3.95	4.01	3.75	3.93	2.44	3.05	2.89	2.70	2.49
Earnings as percentage of sales	3.8%	3.3%	4.3%	4.7%	4.7%	5.7%	4.1	5.3%	5.1%	5.1%	5.0%
Earned on shareowners' equity	12.6%	11.0%	14.8%	15.9%	15.7%	17.5%	11.5%	14.9%	15.0%	14.8%	14.3%
Cash dividends declared	$235.4	$235.2	$234.8	$234.2	$234.6	$216.7	$197.7	$183.1	$177.5	$176.4	$175.5
Dividends declared per common share	2.60	2.60	2.60	2.60	2.60	2.40	2.20	2.05	2.00	2.00	2.00
Market price range per share	94½–60¼	98¼–74⅛	100⅜–80¼	115⅞–82½	120–80	120¼–91	93⅝–78¾	87½–71¾	78½–54¼	80¾–60½	99⅞–70¼
Current assets	3,334.8	3,287.8	3,311.1	3,207.6	3,013.0	2,842.4	$2,543.8	2,321.0	2,024.6	1,859.7	1,846.6
Current liabilities	2,650.3	2,366.7	2,104.3	1.977.4	1,883.2	1,566.8	1,338.9	1,181.9	1,168.7	1,086.6	960.0
Total assets	6,309.9	6,007.5	5,743.8	5,347.2	4,851.7	4,300.4	3,856.0	3,502.5	3,349.9	3,143.4	2,938.8
Total shareowners' equity	2,655.1	2,540.0	2,493.4	2,342.2	2,211.7	2,107.0	1,944.2	1,889.2	1,764.3	1,654.6	1,568.5
Plant and equipment additions	581.4	530.6	514.7	561.7	484.9	332.9	237.7	149.2	173.2	179.7	166.2
Depreciation	334.7	351.3	300.1	280.4	233.4	188.4	170.3	149.4	146.0	131.6	125.1
Total taxes and renegotiation	309.4	313.2	390.5	390.1	409.1	403.8	277.3	331.4	298.7	289.9	234.1
Provision for income taxes	220.6	231.5	312.3	320.5	347.4	352.2	233.8	286.7	254.0	248.9	196.3
Employees' average number worldwide	396,583	410,126	395,691	384,864	375,852	332,991	308,233	297,726	290,682	279,547	236,250

[a]Dollar amounts in millions; per-share amounts in dollars.

ized in the 1930s and 1940s.** Cordiner broke the company down into departments that, as he used to say, "were a size that a man could get his arms around." And what the company would say after giving a man his department was, "Here, take this $50 million department and grow it into $125 million." Then the department would be split into two departments, like an amoeba.

Along with decentralization, Cordiner pushed for expansion of GE's businesses and product lines. With growth and diversity, however, came problems of control. A business historian has assessed Cordiner as follows:

> The case for Cordiner lies in his improvement of GE's numerators and in his creation of a truly remarkable "can-do" organization. He was the champion of volume and diversity and of make rather than buy. He built a company unmatched in American business history in the capacity to pursue those objectives. In the sense of home grown know-how, GE **could** do almost anything; and, in the sense of in-house capacity, GE could do a lot of things, simultaneously.

> But the very expansiveness and evangelism that were Cordiner's strengths were flawed by permissiveness and lack of proportion. "We can do it" too often became "We should do it." For example, massive investments with long payback periods were undertaken simultaneously in nuclear power, aerospace, and computers with a blithe self-confidence in GE's ability to "do-it-ourselves." A sort of "marketing macropia" persisted in which previously constrained market segmentations and product definitions were escalated beyond experience or prudence. For example, "wiring" suddenly becomes "construction materials"; "meters" becomes "measuring devices"; "controls" becomes "automation" and "automation" becomes "computers." Peculiar new rationales are heard: "We should get in now because it will cost us more to get in later"; or, "It's going to cost us more **not** to do it."[3]

---

*For example, as late as 1948 any proposed exempt pay increase that raised a salary to more than $6000 annually had to be sent to New York for the personal signature of the chief executive.

As Fred Borch faced the challenges of leading General Electric in the mid 1960s, internal studies of the company's problems began to proliferate. (Indeed, careful self-examination was and remains a GE characteristic.) One such study set out to give management a tool for evaluating business plans by delineating the key factors associated with profitable results.* Another study undertaken by GE's Growth Council tried to determine how the company could properly position itself to meet its long-time goal of growing faster than the gross national product (GNP). Despite these and other staff studies, profitless growth continued.

In an interview with me, Reginald Jones offered the following diagnosis of the company's problem at the time:

> Our performance reflected poor planning and a poor understanding of the businesses. A major reason for this weakness was the way we were organized. Under the existing structure with functional staff units at the corporate level, business plans only received functional reviews. They were not given a business evaluation.
>
> True, we had a corporate planning department, but they were more concerned with econometric models and environmental forecasting than with hard-headed business plan evaluation. Fortunately, Fred Borch was able to recognize the problem.

To help unravel these problems and to obtain an outside perspective, in 1969 Borch commissioned McKinsey & Company to study the effectiveness of GE's corporate staff and of the planning done at the operating level. He commented on McKinsey's study:

> They were totally amazed at how the company ran as well as it did with the planning that was being done or not being done at various operating levels. In their personal remarks to me over the desk, their conclusions were a lot more pungently expressed than they were in their written report. But they saw some tremendous opportunities for moving the company ahead if we devoted the necessary competence and time to facing up to these, as they saw it, very critical problems.

*This approach eventually led to the PIMS model, which has been made available to industry at large by the Strategic Planning Institute.

In their report, they made two specific recommendations. One was that we recognize that our departments were not really businesses. We had been saying that they were the basic building blocks of the company for many years, but they weren't. They were fractionated and they were parts of larger businesses. The thrust of the recommendation was that we reorganize the company from an operations standpoint and create what they call Strategic Business Units— the terminology stolen from a study we made back in 1957. They gave certain criteria for these and in brief what this amounted to were reasonably self-sufficient businesses that did not meet head-on with other strategic business units in making the major management decisions necessary. They also recommended as part of this that the thirty-three or thirty-five or forty strategic business units report directly to the CEO regardless of the size of the business or the present level in the organization.

Their second recommendation had to do with the formation of group- and corporate-level staff components, and their major recommendation was that we face up to the fact that we were never going to get the longer range work done necessary to progress the company through the '70s, unless we made a radical change in our staff components. The thrust of their recommendation was to separate out the ongoing work necessary to keep General Electric going from the work required to posture the company for the future.[4]

INTRODUCTION OF STRATEGIC PLANNING

After McKinsey made its recommendations, the highest priority on Fred Borch's agenda became the successful introduction of portfolio planning. In pursuing this objective, Borch was highly sensitive to the administrative problems that changes to GE's huge organization would cause, and he was willing to let committees, compromises, and consensus affect the approach and the speed with which portfolio planning was introduced. Thus Borch's first action following the McKinsey report was to establish a task force to make recommendations for implementing McKinsey's suggestions.

The task force spent two intensive months preparing alternatives and recommendations for consideration by the Corporate

Executive Office.* With regard to the staff organization, they agreed with McKinsey's recommendation to restructure GE's corporate staff into two parts. The existing staff units that provided ongoing services to the Corporate Executive Office and to the operating units were grouped as the Corporate Administrative Staff and were to report to a senior vice president. This Corporate Administrative Staff was to deal with functional operational matters. As a counterpart, a Corporate Executive Staff was created to help the CEO plan the future of the General Electric Company. It comprised four staff components—finance, strategic planning, technology, and legal and governance—each headed by a senior vice president.

Establishing Strategic Business Units

While the task force agreed with McKinsey's recommendations with regard to the staff organization, it anticipated several problems in implementing the recommendation to create strategic business units reporting directly to the CEO. One problem was what to do with GE's existing line-reporting structure of groups, divisions, and departments. McKinsey's proposal had been to abandon GE's current organizational structure and to reorganize on the basis of SBUs. The task force was concerned that such a change might seriously jeopardize the successful functioning of GE's operational control system. Fred Borch commented:

> We decided that their [McKinsey's] recommendations on both the operating front and the staff front conceptually were very sound. They hit right at the nut of the problem, but the implementation that they recommended just wouldn't fly as far as General Electric was concerned. . . . We accepted about 100% of their conceptual contribution and virtually none of their implementation recommendations.

---

*The Corporate Executive Office included the chief executive officer and the vice chairmen. GE usually had two or three vice chairmen.

Another administrative problem of adopting an SBU structure was that it would radically change established power and status relationships among important managers. An executive explained Borch's dilemma:

> The company was operating with 190 departments, each headed by an important person. If we were to change immediately to an organization of forty-five strategic business units, Borch would have had the unpleasant task of demoting 145 managers.

To avoid these administrative problems, Borch decided to superimpose the SBU structure on the existing line-reporting structure. For ongoing operations, managers would report according to the group/division/department structure. Only units designated SBUs, however, would prepare strategic plans. Thus, at General Electric, as at the Dexter Corporation, administrative considerations had a significant impact on the designation of business units.

As shown in Figure 10.1, a group, division, or department could be designated an SBU. This overlay of a strategic planning structure on the operating structure resulted in a variety of reporting relationships. When a department was named an SBU, for example, the department manager would report directly to the CEO for planning purposes but to a division manager for operating purposes. GE managers expressed the opinion that this approach provided the company with the best of both worlds—tight operational control on a comprehensive basis and planning at the relevant levels. It also reduced the necessity of reassigning or demoting those department- or group-level managers who were not given SBU designations. One manager commented:

> There was always the possibility that a group executive of a group that was not an SBU would feel that his status had been diminished. But this didn't happen. Even though the department or division SBU managers were to report directly to the CEO for planning, they would normally review their plans with the group executive.

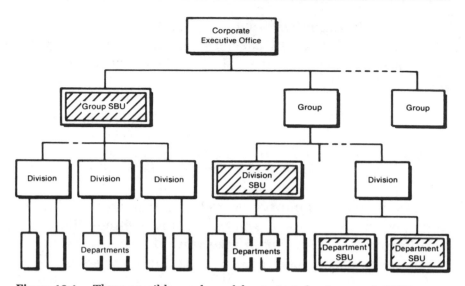

Figure 10.1. Three possible overlays of the strategic business unit (SBU) structure at the General Electric Company

> In theory, the intervening layers of management were supposed to
> be transparent for planning purposes and opaque for control pur-
> poses. In practice, they were translucent for both. In a sense, we
> loosened the SBU structure to allow personal influence and power
> to shape the important strategic decisions.

Identifying SBUs was another problem for Borch and the task
force. The task force could readily agree on the characteristics of
an SBU,* and about 80% of the SBUs could be easily identified
and agreed on. The other 20% required considerable judgment, not
because of difficulties in applying the technical criteria for SBUs
but because of administrative considerations. A staff planner who
worked on SBU designations explained:

---

*The general characteristics of an SBU were defined as follows: a unique set of
competitors, a unique business mission, a competitor in external markets (as
opposed to an internal supplier), the ability to accomplish integrated strategic
planning, and the ability "to call the shots" on the variables crucial to the success
of the business.

In some of these cases, we had small departments that were in trouble that Borch was reluctant to lose control of by not granting them SBU status. In other cases, there were units that clearly should be designated SBUs but that had weak managers. In some of these instances, it took until the end of 1972 to get the SBU designation straight, and often the final choice was based on Borch's "comfort index" with the business and with the manager running the business.

The establishment and designation of SBUs, then, was shaped by administrative as well as strategic considerations. Whereas McKinsey & Company provided General Electric with a strategic justification of an SBU structure, its implementation ideas were abandoned in favor of an approach that was consistent with Fred Borch's management approach. The introduction of portfolio planning took over two years and was most sensitive to administrative constraints.

Defining a Business Plan

Even with the reduction in the number of business plans from 190 departments to 43 SBUs, the CEO faced a formidable task of reviewing all of the plans. One GE manager noted that "Borch had a sense that he wasn't looking for lots of data on each business unit, but really wanted 15 terribly important and significant pages of data and analysis."

To deal with this problem, three of the group vice presidents were asked to work with three different consulting companies (Arthur D. Little, Boston Consulting Group, and McKinsey & Company) to find a way to compress all of the strategic planning data into the most effective presentation possible. It was from GE's collaborative effort with McKinsey that the development of the nine-block summary of business and investment strategy came. (This portfolio planning technique was described in Chapter 1 as the company position/industry attractiveness screen, so it will not be described again here.) It is significant to note that this portfolio planning technique was developed as a way to address the administrative problem of how to compress information for a busy CEO, rather than as a rigorous technical tool of strategic analysis. One GE executive commented to me about two reasons why the nine-block summary subsequently was so enthusiastically embraced in General Electric:

> The nine-block summary had tremendous appeal to us, not only because it compressed a lot of data but also because it contained enough subjective evaluation to appeal to the thinking of GE management.

The only instructions for the SBU manager concerning the content of a business plan was a listing of the topics that had to be covered. For example, the topics to be covered in the 1973 strategic plans were:

1. The identification and formulation of environmental assumptions of strategic importance.
2. The identification and in-depth analysis of competitors, including assumptions about their probable strategies.
3. The analysis of the SBU's own resources.
4. The development and evaluation of strategy alternatives.
5. The preparation of the SBU Strategic Plan, including estimates of capital spending for the next five years.
6. The preparation of the SBU Operating Plan, which detailed the next ensuing year of the SBU Strategic Plan.

Reginald Jones, who became GE's Chairman and Chief Executive Officer in December 1972, added a proviso concerning how the plans were to be presented:

> At our General Management Conference in January 1973, I stirred up quite a few members of that audience when I said that I expected every SBU manager to be able to stand before a peer group and, without benefit of visual aids, give a clear and concise state-

ment of his strategic plan. And that every manager reporting to him should fully understand that statement and be able to explain it to his troops. I meant it. When that happens, then you can say that planning has become a way of life.

Staffing the Planning Effort

With the new SBU planning approach in place, there remained the question of how to staff the effort. Two important actions were taken. First, each SBU manager was required to hire an SBU strategic planner. Because of the limited number of experienced strategic planners in the company at that time, many of the people filling these posts were hired from outside the company, an unusual practice for GE. Over time, many of the SBUs developed planning staffs and the planning positions were filled internally. By 1980, there were approximately 200 senior-level planners in General Electric. About half of these were career planners, while the other half were rotating through the position as part of their career development.

To assist both the SBU general managers and the strategic planners, both groups were required to attend special strategic planning seminars that were set up at GE's Management Development Center in Crotonville, New York. Not only were all department and division general managers (more than 240 in total) required to take a one-week course, but they were also given a metal suitcase with a slide-and-tape show to present to their subordinates after the course. The strategic planners were required to take a two-week course.

PLANNING IN JONES' EARLY YEARS: 1972-1976

When Reginald Jones became GE's CEO in December of 1972 at the age of 53, he inherited a company that had the can-do attitude of success in all of the businesses in which it competed. Indeed, as embodied in its slogan, "Progress is our most important product,"

General Electric's institutional strategy had as its cornerstone a belief in and a reliance on technology, entrepreneurship, and innovation. Yet as the former chief financial officer of the company, Jones was well aware that many of GE's new efforts had not earned adequate financial returns. Thus the item at the top of Jones' agenda in the early years of his tenure was to improve GE's rate of return without jeopardizing its institutional strategy of innovation.

One way for GE to achieve higher rates of return, as shown in Chapter 4, was to divest marginal businesses. Indeed, Jones had already done this in May 1970 when, as GE's chief financial officer, he negotiated the sale of GE's mainframe computer business. Jones' vigorous backing of strategic planning and nine-block analysis provided additional impetus for exiting weak businesses. During his entire tenure a total of 73 product lines, including vacuum cleaners, fans, phonographs, and heart pacemakers, were divested. A GE manager commented on how the combination of portfolio planning, Jones' track record, and Jones' priorities led to divestitures:

> Whether the planning system led to the [computer] divestiture was irrelevant. The appearance was there nonetheless. From then on it became fashionable to prune businesses. And Jones' subsequent promotion gave even more credibility to those managers who were willing to face up to the fact that certain businesses had to be exited.

> The planning system was just another tool that enabled a manager to face up to certain inevitabilities. Prior to this we had really operated with a "floating J curve." In other words, businesses would forecast two or three years of flat or declining profitability, but then all of the numbers would point upwards. What Jones was able to do with the computer business and what strategic planning revealed was that the floating J curve was a fantasy.

While less profitable businesses were being discontinued, GE's growth businesses and some new businesses received a greater proportion of capital funds. For example, GE's technical systems and materials businesses received considerable funding and accounted for almost 25% of total earnings by 1977, compared with less than 10% in 1970.

Lest we exaggerate the impact of strategic planning on GE's business mix, it is essential to point out that Reg Jones' most significant strategic move, the 1976 acquisition of Utah International,* was not made because of analysis provided by GE's portfolio approach to strategic planning. Jones explained:

> This was sort of an ad hoc decision that came about because of a fortuitous opportunity developing. . . . It is true that when our strategic planning was put in place and we began to look for areas of growth and diversification that mining was not one that came to us from our own strategic planning exercises. It did develop because Ed Littlefield [Utah's chairman] was a valued member of our Board of Directors. . . .

Thus in the first five years of Reg Jones' tenure as CEO of General Electric, the major impact of portfolio planning had been to encourage the divestiture of low-potential, low-return businesses and to provide a disciplined and consistent approach to strategic planning throughout the company. Although portfolio planning also led to the increased funding of some growth businesses, GE's entry into the natural resources business took place outside the realm of the strategic planning system.

During this period, Jones' management approach was to deal directly with the substance of strategic decisions. Jones knew what his objectives were and usually was cognizant of administrative constraints when implementing them. Rather than unilaterally divesting businesses, he was able to use portfolio planning as a tool to get managers to recommend, on their own, which businesses to divest. But as in the case of the Utah acquisition, he was also willing to act unilaterally. Indeed as Jones became more firmly entrenched in his position, he became less constrained by

---

*At the time it was the largest acquisition ever to have taken place in the United States.

administrative considerations. For example, by 1975 GE ceased to operate with the separate operating and planning organizations that Borch had created. The problem of dealing with those department managers who had not been named SBU managers was greatly mitigated because over time, numerous opportunities had arisen to reassign managers. During this period, then, GE was able to use the portfolio approach to improve top management's ability to allocate resources within the company.

By 1977, General Electric had already gained a considerable reputation for its planning skill, and financial performance was at record levels.[5] Return on equity, for example, reached 19.4%, its highest mark since the 1950s. Within the company, the portfolio approach to strategic planning had become a way of life, as reported in the following excerpt from a December 1974 internal audit of strategic planning:

> The overwhelming feeling is that strategic planning has become ingrained in General Electric. 80% felt there would be no slippage and 16% only minor slippage if corporate requirements for SP (strategic planning) were removed.

PLANNING IN JONES' LATER YEARS: 1977–1981

Despite the success and acceptance of strategic planning, in 1977 Reg Jones made major modifications in GE's approach to portfolio planning. These changes, which met with considerable success, were made because of changes in Jones' agenda and management approach, because of some of the administrative consequences of having used portfolio planning, and to address certain issues that the portfolio approach overlooked.

The Sector Organization

At the General Management Conference in January 1977, Reg Jones announced his intention "to revise GE's strategic planning system and to establish a 'sector' organization structure as the pivotal concept for the redesign effort." There were several reasons for this change. The first was an administrative consequence of using the portfolio approach. Namely, Jones had experienced difficulty in reviewing all 43 SBU plans. He explained:

> *Right from the start of SBU planning in 1972, the vice chairmen and I tried to review each plan in great detail. This effort took untold hours and placed tremendous burden on the Corporate Executive Office. After a while I began to realize that no matter how hard we would work, we could not achieve the necessary in-depth understanding of the forty-odd SBU plans. Somehow the review burden had to be carried on more shoulders.*

Creating the sector structure was Jones' way to spread the review load. The sector was defined as a new level of management that represented a macro-business or industry area.* The sector executive, who was to serve as the GE spokesman for that industry, was to be responsible for providing management direction to the member SBUs, for reviewing the SBU strategic plans, and for integrating the SBU strategies into a sector strategic plan, which would focus heavily on development opportunities transcending SBU lines but still within the scope of the sector. The Corporate Executive Office would thereafter focus its review on the strategic plans of the six sectors. Thus the sector organization had the effect of reducing the review burden on the CEO from forty-three to six strategic plans. Such an approach runs counter to the conventional wisdom about portfolio planning—that the CEO needs to review all of the businesses in order to allocate resources effectively. But the sector approach does address the administrative

---

*Robert Frederick, the executive who had been assigned the tasks of introducing the sector structure and of making it work, explained the new nomenclature: "We picked the word 'sector' because no one knew what it meant. In that way, there would be no preconceived notions of what the sectors would do."

realities that a CEO has limited time and typically chooses to focus on a few key issues.

The second set of reasons for the adoption of the sector organization had to do with shifts in Jones' agenda and management approach that were occurring at this time. Whereas in the early years of his tenure Jones' highest priority was returning GE to financial strength, by 1977 his priorities were shifting to his role as a business spokesman in Washington, D.C., to the need to revitalize GE's technologic base and product development, and to the necessity of identifying a successor.

Jones' Washington activities included cochairing the Business Roundtable and becoming one of President Carter's closest contacts and advisers within the business community. The time Jones devoted to these activities limited his time for internal GE matters. By giving increased responsibilities to six sector executives, Jones was able to reduce GE's need for his time.

The creation of the sectors was also consistent with Jones' priority that GE's major strategic need was to revitalize its technology and to develop new businesses. Despite the advantages of portfolio planning, planning activities that were focused on SBUs more often resulted in divestiture recommendations than in bold business initiatives. Reg Jones commented:

> In 1976, I commissioned a companywide study of our strengths, weaknesses, and needs in technology. The findings—sixteen volumes of them—triggered a technological renaissance in G.E. We stepped up our R&D budgets, built up our electronic capabilities, and reoriented our recruiting and training activities.
>
> The sectors helped too. Conceptually, the SBUs were expected to develop new business opportunities by extending into contiguous product/market areas. The sectors were expected to develop new SBUs by diversifying within their macro-industry scopes.

The final shift in Jones' agenda that led to the adoption of the sector organization was the need to identify a successor. By creating six very high-level sector executive positions, Jones was able to structure a situation in which six individuals would have equal opportunities to demonstrate their talents. Reg Jones explained:

> I had a personal road map of the future and knew when I wanted to retire. Time was moving on, and I could see a need to put the key candidates for my job under a spotlight for the Board to view. The sector executive positions would provide the visibility.

> The men were assigned to sectors with businesses different from their past experience. I did this not only to broaden these individuals but also to leaven the businesses by introducing new bosses who had different perspectives. For example, major appliances had long been run by managers who had grown up in the business. I put Welch, whose previous experience had been with high-technology plastics, in charge to see if he could introduce new approaches.

These shifts in Jones' agenda were accompanied by a change in his management approach. By virtue of the fact that he was spending so much time in Washington and that he was giving so much responsibility to the sector executives, almost of necessity Jones had to manage the processes by which strategies were being developed rather than to determine the outcomes of strategic decisions directly by himself.

Corporate Challenges and Strategy Integration

The second change that Jones made to GE's strategic planning system in 1977 was to establish additional mechanisms by which top management could affect the plans of the SBUs and the sectors. These mechanisms took the form of specific corporate challenges that each SBU and sector had to address and plans for the resources and activities that were common to all GE businesses. Both of these mechanisms are reviewed here, but first it is important to consider the shortcomings of the portfolio approach that motivated them.

The primary concerns that gave rise to the corporate challenges and integrating mechanisms were the growing lack of consistency and cohesiveness among the many SBU plans and the inability of the Chief Executive Officer to affect much more than the basic mission and investment intentions of the SBUs. Indeed while portfolio planning techniques provide corporate managers with a powerful tool for shaping SBU strategic objectives and investment plans, they do not address specific strategic problems such as productivity, technology, quality, or the problem of integrating the activities of similar SBUs. Reg Jones commented on the problems that arise when the corporate role in portfolio planning is limited to defining strategic mandates and investment priorities:

> At the strategic level, we seemed to be moving in all directions with no sense of focus on what I saw as major opportunities and threats for the 1980s. For example, I saw a need to push forward on the international front, a need to move from our electromechanical technology to electronics, and a need to respond to the problems of productivity. We needed a way to challenge our managers to respond to these pressing issues in an integrated fashion.

To provide corporate direction and impetus with respect to such issues, GE introduced the concept of corporate planning challenges. As shown in Figure 10.2, the planning challenges set

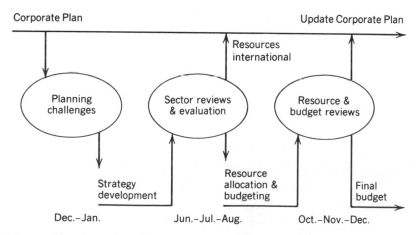

Figure 10.2. Annual planning cycle of the General Electric Company

the stage for the annual strategic planning cycle. Each year the CEO would issue a number of specific challenges that had to be addressed in the strategic plans of the SBUs and the sectors. For example, a 1980 corporate challenge called for SBUs and sectors to plan for a productivity improvement appropriate for their industry to counter worldwide competitive threats. The productivity target for GE as a whole was set for 6%.

In addition to the CEO as a source of challenges, the restructured management system included two new approaches for generating planning challenges. One element aimed at fostering GE's international activities, the other at integrating GE's planning for critical resources.

International Sector. To increase the importance and the visibility of international operations in GE, Jones set it up as a sector. It was, however, to play a special role among sectors: In addition to preparing a sector plan for GE's overseas affiliates, the International Sector also was given responsibility for fostering and integrating international business for General Electric as a whole.

A subsequent effort to integrate electric iron manufacturing on a worldwide basis illustrates one of the roles that the International Sector was intended to play. The SBU responsible for irons had developed a newly designed iron, which it planned for production in a single small country. At International Sector urging, the SBU reconsidered and ultimately decided on rationalized multi-country production in three countries, including two larger countries with International Sector affiliates. This approach improved cost and market share potentials in affiliate countries as well as cost effectiveness on a total GE System basis. This intervention led to an internal joint venture for irons between the International Sector and the SBU to share risks and rewards on a worldwide basis.

Resource Planning. Corporate management's concerns with GE's handling of critical resources were to be dealt with through another companywide integrating mechanism. For this purpose, senior corporate staff executives were given responsibility "for an objective assessment of key resources and the identification of issues impacting the company's strategic strengths." These assessments with respect to financial resources, human resources, technology resources, and production resources would lead to planning challenges to the sectors and the SBUs wherever practices needed to be improved.

Planning for human resources illustrated how this approach was to work. The vice president in charge of this planning described two of the issues he had subsequently raised for management consideration:

> One of the major human resources issues GE has had to face had to do with the potential impact of transferring work and jobs to overseas locations. This practice has important implications for the company, for the employees, and for the communities involved which had to be thought through beforehand. Another important issue had to do with GE's image as it relates to recruiting college graduates. In the next few years GE has to hire some 2,800 scientists and engineers, competing with some glamorous firms for the good people.

Results of the Changes

The results of the changes in strategic planning that were initiated in 1977 were generally very favorable. As shown in Table 10.2, GE's financial performance remained at record levels in the 1978–1980 period. The sector organization became firmly entrenched as part of GE's management system. The sectors provided an intermediate level at which SBU plans could be reviewed intensively, and it also reduced the workload on the CEO. Reg Jones explained:

> The sector approach turned out to be very successful. It even exceeded my expectations. I could look at six planning books and understand them well enough to ask the right questions. I could not do that before.

TABLE 10.2. STATISTICAL SUMMARY FOR THE GENERAL ELECTRIC COMPANY, 1971–1980

Item[a]	Year 1980	1979	1978	1977	1976	1975	1974	1973	1972	1971[b]
Sales of products and services	$24,959	$22,461	$19,654	$17,519	$15,697	$14,105	$13,918	$11,945	$10,474	$9,557
Earnings before income taxes and minority interest	2,493	2,391	2,153	1,889	1,627	1,174	1,181	1,130	963	847
Taxes	958	953	894	773	668	460	458	457	385	333
Net earnings	1,514	1,409	1,230	1,088	931	688	705	661	573	510
Earnings per common share	6.65	6.20	5.39	4.79	4.12	3.07	3.16	2.97	2.57	2.30
Dividends declared per common share	2.95	2.75	2.50	2.10	1.70	1.60	1.60	1.50	1.40	1.38
Earnings as percentage of sales	6.1%	6.3%	6.3%	6.2%	5.9%	4.9%	5.1%	5.5%	5.5%	5.3%
Earned on average share-owners' equity	19.5%	20.2%	19.6%	19.4%	18.9%	15.7%	17.8%	18.4%	17.5%	17.2%
Dividends	$670	$624	$570	$477	$333	$293	$291	$273	$ 255	$250
Market price range per share	63–44	55⅛–45	57⅝–43⅝	57¼–47⅜	59¼–46	52⅞–32⅜	65–30	75⅞–55	73–58¼	66½–46½
Current assets	9,883	9,384	8,755	7,865	6,685	5,750	5,334	4,597	4,057	3,700
Current liabilities	7,592	6,872	6,175	5,417	4,605	4,163	4,032	3,588	2,921	2,894
Shareowners' equity	8,200	7,362	6,587	5,943	5,253	4,617	4,172	3,774	3,420	3,106
Total assets	18,511	16,644	15,036	13,697	12,050	10,741	10,220	9,089	8,051	7,472
Property, plant, and equipment additions	1,948	1,262	1,055	823	740	588	813	735	501	711
Employees, average number worldwide	402,000	405,000	401,000	384,000	380,000	380,000	409,000	392,000	373,000	366,000

[a]Dollar amounts in millions; per-share amounts in dollars.

[b]Two-for-one stock split.

The sector executives were also given considerable leverage in the allocation of resources within their sector. For example, each year GE's profit target was determined by a corporate staff analysis of what profit each SBU was expected to achieve. Prior to the creation of the sector organization, each SBU developed a budget to achieve its profit target. After the sector organization was created, the corporate staff still prepared SBU profit targets. But they were then consolidated, so that each sector was given a total profit objective, which the sector executive allocated to his SBUs in the proportions considered most appropriate. This change in planning and budgeting procedures represented a significant shift in the degree to which resource allocation was being administered from the corporate level of GE's organization.

The appointment of six sector executives also facilitated the identification of Jones' successor. In 1979, three of the sector executives were elevated to the position of vice chairman and were named to GE's Board of Directors. This narrowed the field of potential successors and gave the Board an opportunity to evaluate the candidates on a closer basis. In December 1980, Reg Jones announced that, effective April 1, 1981, Jack Welch would become the CEO of the General Electric Company. Jones took considerable pride in the way he had handled the task of choosing his successor:

> Leaving a company with a strong management is the most important thing a CEO can do. That's why I get so much satisfaction from the way my successor was chosen. We were able to involve the Board and objectively appraise the candidates over a period of years, not months. And not only did we get a strong new CEO but we also got a strong new team of managers to lead the company.

The corporate challenges and strategy integration efforts also met with considerable success, as the company had made considerable progress in addressing some of the challenges. For example, Reg Jones pointed with similar pride to the company's response to the technology challenge:

> These past few years we have pressed hard the challenge to change the company's basic technology from electromechanical to elec-

tronics. Today we have a true companywide effort to apply the new micro-electronics and the related information-based technologies to every possible product, service, and process in GE.

Despite this progress, General Electric, toward the end of Reg Jones' administration, was still searching for additional ways to stimulate growth and entrepreneurship within the context of its strategic planning system. It was this issue that Jones' successor would have to resolve.

STRATEGIC PLANNING UNDER JACK WELCH

The selection of 44-year-old Jack Welch to become General Electric's CEO reflected the increasing importance that Reg Jones and the Board of Directors were placing on GE's needs for business development and technologic leadership. These objectives are at the core of GE's institutional strategy and were never ignored during the 1970s. But in the aftermath of GE's exit from the computer mainframe business, the emphasis on increasing financial performance may have supplanted the needs for business development and technologic leadership. By the end of the 1970s under Reg Jones' direction, this emphasis was being reversed through a revision of GE's approach to strategic planning that would shift the focus to growth opportunities and challenges.

Jack Welch, a Ph.D. chemical engineer, personified this renewed emphasis on business development. Early in his career Welch had been responsible for GE's very successful entry into the specialty materials (plastics) business. By 1980, this business accounted for over $1 billion of sales. As a group vice president, Welch had been responsible for GE's highly successful entry into computed tomography scanners, a business in which GE now occupies a worldwide leadership position. Throughout his career, Welch was known as an entrepreneurial operating manager who was decisive and willing to take risks.

At General Electric's shareholder's meeting in April 1981, Jack Welch discussed his objective for the company:

A decade from now we would like General Electric to be perceived as a unique, high-spirited, entrepreneurial enterprise ... a company known around the world for its unmatched level of excellence. We want General Electric to be the most profitable highly diversified company on earth, with world quality leadership in every one of its product lines.

To achieve this objective, it was clear, Welch would continue to use the same management approach that had already marked his career. For example, Welch was a strong believer in placing maximum responsibility with line managers and minimizing the restraints on their actions. And although Welch was deeply involved in the selection and appraisal of GE's managers, he did not get very involved in the formulation of specific strategies. He commented:

I am the ultimate believer in people first, strategies second. To me strategy starts with the person you hire. If a business lacks a good strategy, then put in charge of the business someone who will develop one. If that person becomes the owner of the strategy and is given responsibility for acheiving it, that's the way to play the game.

I changed the rules when I became CEO. Every department manager and up now has to come through my office, in terms of the slate process. I meet them. I want to get a feel for them, know them. I am involved in the selection and compensation of 125 people in detail, and 500 with a pass-off.

One manifestation of Welch's objectives and approach was an emphasis on "internal ventures" as a way to focus attention on new product development. Each sector was encouraged to foster ventures that would bring GE into new market and product areas. By late 1981, there were at least 60 new business ventures within the company. Even though most of these ventures had been relieved of profit pressure during their start-up, the ventures and their managers were still very much under a spotlight. Jack Welch explained:

Today we need entrepreneurs who are willing to take well-considered business risks and, at the same time, know how to work in harmony with a larger business entity. . . .

We have a section of the manpower book on ventures. What are the twelve embryo businesses you have in your sector that are being fueled by what twelve people? The ventures are far less important than the products of the processes, which are the people. By having high visibility on a dozen people—each having their own P&L statement, their own game, competing against the world—we get a chance to look at how they perform.

Welch's emphasis on making operating managers responsible for strategy also had implications for GE's planning system. For example, Welch had resumed Reg Jones' earlier practice of reviewing the plans and strategies of all of GE's SBUs. In place of the larger meetings held in the past, Welch involved only the SBU manager and the responsible vice chairman in the review. He directed the review around key issues for each business and not around comprehensive strategic documentation. For example, one issue that was raised repeatedly in these reviews was what each SBU would be doing to benefit GE in 1990. Jack Welch explained the reasons for these changes:

One of the things that's happened is with our planning system. It was dynamite when we first put it in. The thinking was fresh; the form was little— the format got no points—it was idea-oriented. Then we hired a head of planning and he hired two vice presidents and then he hired a planner, and then the books got thicker, and the printing got more sophisticated and the covers got harder and the drawings got better. The meetings kept getting larger. Nobody can say anything with sixteen or eighteen people there.

So one of the things that we have put into place is a way to achieve more candor, more constructive conflict. So we've gone to what we're going to call CEO meetings* where the three of us will have

*Corporate Executive Office: Chairman J. Welch, Vice Chairman J. Burlingame, and Vice Chairman E. Hood.

meetings with SBU managers, one on three, two on three, in a small
room.

The reviews that Jack Welch conducted with the SBU managers
were intensive and comprehensive. By the end of 1981, these
CEO – SBU strategy-setting sessions had largely supplanted many
of the more formal planning mechanisms that had been instituted
in recent years. In place of a portfolio planning system built
around nine-block analyses, Welch's approach to planning was
built around those general managers who were responsible for
running GE's businesses.

To help the company focus on specific and cross-sector opportunities, within six months of becoming CEO Welch instituted
the first major change in GE's sector management structure since
its establishment in 1977. As reported in GE, the changes reflected
"the Company's current capabilities and active pursuit of growing
opportunities in the service businesses." In this connection, two
new sectors were added: (1) a Technical Systems Sector, to focus
on "the electronics-based businesses critically involved in GE's
'factory of the future' strategy" and to include businesses intensively using microelectronics, such as industrial electronics, advanced microelectronics, medical systems, and aerospace; and (2)
a Services and Materials Sector to manage the high-growth Engineered Materials Group and to forge new linkages in financial and
information services by bringing together GE Credit and the Information Services Division. Jack Welch explained some of the reasons for the reorganization:

> *Why did we reorganize this time? Because GE Information Services,*
> *with all their networking, and GE Credit were in two different*
> *places under two different sector people. We were convinced there*
> *was some synergy there in tying networking to financial services.*
> *The best way to do that is to combine them in a sector and let the*
> *sector executive figure it out.*
>
> *In the case of microelectronics and the factory of the future, we had*
> *a microelectronics lab in one sector, the research lab in another*
> *sector, and two businesses with enormous microelectronic cap-*

ability, aerospace and medical systems, that were in different sectors. We put all the microelectronics activities together and we do not have a rational solution. Some day we will look like geniuses because we packaged it just perfectly. Right now, all we know is they are all working on similar projects, fighting tough market environments, and needing lots of technical capability. So we are putting them all together so that we can try to address their common needs and problems.

At the end of 1981, I completed my research at General Electric. By that time, Welch's agenda and management approach had been clearly revealed. Equally clear was the fact that an agenda of growth and business development and an emphasis on the people needed to make strategy a reality left much less room for reliance on portfolio planning techniques.

SUMMARY

The description I have offered of General Electric's approach to portfolio planning is one of a system that has changed several times during the past decade. Table 10.3 traces these changes and shows their relationship to the four forces that shape strategic processes. Yet even though all four of the forces help to explain GE's modifications to portfolio planning, it is the agendas and management approaches of GE's CEOs that seem to have had the greatest impact on how strategies were formed and implemented.

When Fred Borch introduced portfolio planning techniques in the early 1970s, he chose to pay close attention to administrative considerations and to institute changes slowly. Borch, who was facing serious financial constraints, was willing to modify the portfolio approach to gain the support of the organization for his efforts.

When Reg Jones became CEO in December 1972, his agenda and approach were different from Borch's. Jones' highest priority was to improve the company's financial performance, and he became actively involved in assuring that his objectives were being im-

TABLE 10.3. FORCES SHAPING STRATEGY FORMULATION AND IMPLEMENTATION AT GENERAL ELECTRIC COMPANY

CEO, Time Period	CEO Agenda	CEO Strategic Management Approach	Financial Resources	Administrative Considerations	Implications for Use of Portfolio Planning
Borch, 1969–1972	Introduce and gain acceptance of portfolio planning	Manage processes; give high attention to administrative constraints	Constrained	Need to overcome resistance to planning by a large, entrenched organization	Introduce slowly; modify approach, especially regarding SBU definition and reporting relationships, in order to gain acceptance
Jones, 1972–1976	Improve financial performance	Manage outcomes; give varying degrees of attention to administrative constraints	Constrained	Need for organization to face up to divestment decisions	Use for internal resource allocations

| Jones, 1977–1981 | Serve as business spokesman in turbulent economic time; revitalize GE's technologic base; identify a successor | Manage processes | Plentiful | Impossibility of reviewing all SBU plans at CEO level in meaningful way; need to ensure fair race for succession | Modify approach; create sectors; create six separate portfolios and move strategic processes down one level; challenges overcome blind spots of portfolio planning |
| Welch, 1981–present | Work toward growth, innovation, and entrepreneurship | Emphasize identification of strong managers; give less attention to administrative constraints; manage processes | Very plentiful | Need to stimulate innovation in a large organization | Loosen reliance on portfolio planning; broaden SBU definitions to identify opportunities; focus SBU reviews on opportunities and people rather than on nine-block analysis |

plemented. Portfolio planning techniques, particularly the industry attractiveness/business position screens, were vigorously implemented, and the CEO personally reviewed all 43 SBU plans and was intimately involved in resource allocation to the SBUs.

By 1977, GE was producing a considerable cash flow from its operating units, and financial performance was at record levels. Reg Jones' agenda accordingly changed from an emphasis on financial performance to GE's underlying technologic strength. Equally important, Jones began to spend more of his time on national political issues and within the company was concerned with arranging for an orderly succession of management. These shifts in Jones' agenda and in GE's financial performance led to a planning system in which considerable resource allocation and strategy formulation responsibilities were vested in the sector executives, and in which the CEO's major role was to identify common challenges facing all of the company's businesses.

By 1981, GE was in an even stronger financial position but was still in need of approaches to planning that would foster the continued growth and innovation that would be needed in the future. The new CEO, Jack Welch, placed these items at the top of his agenda and involved himself personally in their achievement. As Jones had done early in his tenure, Welch involved himself deeply in the review of SBU plans. But, unlike Jones, who had focused on financial performance and divestiture, Welch focused on determining what each SBU could become over the next decade. Whereas Jones had created sectors to reduce his workload and to facilitate management succession, Welch realigned the sectors and created one new sector to focus the company's SBUs on specific areas of common opportunity.

In my view, General Electric's approach to strategic planning well deserves the publicity and recognition that it has received, not because the company has been the most vigorous and persistent in the implementation of portfolio planning techniques but because it has been able to revise and abandon some techniques and to create new ones to respond to the changing agendas and strategic management approach of its chief executives.

11

The Memorex Corporation: 1961–1971

A CASE STUDY OF WIDELY DIFFERENTIATED RESOURCE ALLOCATION

The case studies of the Dexter Corporation and the General Electric Company have chronicled how those two companies amended the portfolio approach to accommodate administrative considerations, financial constraints, and the agenda and management approach of the CEO. But because they did amend the approach, the case studies suggest only some of the administrative issues posed by the use of portfolio planning techniques. To uncover more of these administrative issues, it is necessary to study a company that more sharply differentiated the allocation of resources to its businesses.

During the mid and late 1960s, the Memorex Corporation vigorously managed itself as a portfolio of businesses that had vastly different growth prospects. As a result, resources were allocated on a widely differentiated basis to the divisions, and incentives and controls were sharply skewed, to encourage the divisions with greater growth potential. Because these actions are so consis-

213

tent with the use of portfolio planning techniques to facilitate resource allocation, our study of the Memorex Corporation enables us to identify many of the administrative issues associated with this approach.

A word of caution, however, is also in order. By the early 1970s, the Memorex Corporation suffered severe financial losses. While to some extent these losses can be attributed to the company's lack of responsiveness to the administrative problems posed by differentiated resource allocation, there were other causes, such as a risky financing strategy, questionable accounting practices, a difficult economic and competitive environment, and simple mismanagement. The purpose of this case study, however, is not to determine why Memorex experienced so many difficulties; rather it is only to spotlight the administrative issues and problems that arose after the company sharply skewed the allocation of resources and incentives to its operating divisions.

EARLY SUCCESSES: 1961–1965

The Memorex Corporation was founded in early 1961 by Laurence Spitters, Donald Eldredge, W. L. Noon, and B. Challman.* The purpose of the company was to manufacture precision magnetic tape for use with data processing equipment. With the growth of the computer industry in the 1950s, the demand for more advanced computer tape was increasing rapidly. Although 3M dominated the industry, the founders of Memorex reasoned that, if they could produce higher quality tape, there would be considerable demand for their product.

The three founders of Memorex who remained with the business worked extremely closely to get the company started, but they also carefully divided their responsibilities. Donald Eldredge took responsibility for developing the tape product; W. L. Noon was responsible for the construction and development of a manu-

*Challman resigned in June 1962.

facturing capability; and Laurence Spitters, who became president and treasurer, was responsible for raising the capital to finance the company. Memorex's founders provided the initial capitalization of $12,500 in February 1961. By April 1961, Spitters had arranged for a private placement that yielded $600,000 in capital.

Even with this financing, the founders of Memorex faced numerous problems and risks. Laurence Spitters has testified:

Twelve thousand five hundred dollars doesn't sound like a lot of money. I didn't have a lot of money. And that was the risk, but that wasn't the major risk.

I think the major risk was the career risk. I think all of us were doing very well in industry, and, . . . had we continued in industry in the normal mode, I think most of us could have expected to graduate to one of the higher levels of industrial management.

The risk is that, when you try a new venture and you fail, you not only forego the opportunity that you might have had, but you penalize yourself because, if you re-enter an industry, you come down at a lower rung on the ladder, and that was a risk.

There's also a risk in terms of the families. My recollection is that there were 20 children under the age of 14 or 15 among the founders, and when you are not working for salary there's a little bit of concern about doing that, and you know the kind of problems, everybody knows the kind of problems that that can engender. So there was a risk of that.[1]

In addition to the career and financial risks, the founders of Memorex were not necessarily assured that they would be able either to develop or to produce a product of the quality that they envisioned. Indeed by mid 1962, they had exhausted their initial capital and had not produced even one reel of commercially usable magnetic tape. Product and manufacturing development were taking longer and requiring more money than had originally been planned.

In September 1962, Laurence Spitters was able to raise an additional $600,000 of capital to assure that Memorex would be able to develop and produce its product. Profits followed quickly. Although Memorex lost about $1 million during 1961 and 1962, in 1963 the company reported a profit of $454,000. As shown in Table 11.1, in 1965 sales reached $13 million and pretax earnings were close to $2.5 million.

Reasons for Success

There were many reasons for Memorex's early success. In terms of its business strategy, Memorex had correctly identified a need for a high-quality tape product and was able to produce it. Indeed the name *Memorex* was an abbreviation of the words *memory excellence*. To distribute its product, Memorex built its own sales organization to sell directly to end users. Admittedly, direct selling was an expensive way to do business, but as a high-quality producer Memorex was able to distinguish itself from its competitors by virtue of the technical knowledge and service of its sales personnel.

Memorex's early success can also be attributed to its focus and to the way in which the firm was managed. During this period, the company focused on a very limited set of objectives in a single line of business and had the complete support of the management team. Laurence Spitters commented:

> The distinguishing characteristic of Memorex's management during the past six years is that we have had well-defined objectives; we know what we do well and how best to exploit our capabilities. We have avoided going off in many directions and have concentrated our interests in a field of special competence.[2]

The average age of Memorex's top 15 managers in 1965 was about 40. Despite their aggressiveness, these managers had worked closely together as a team to create Memorex's success, and all had been awarded stock options. When Memorex made the first public offering of its shares in March 1965 at $25 per share, many of these managers became millionaires.

TABLE 11.1. FINANCIAL PERFORMANCE OF MEMOREX CORPORATION, 1961–1965

Performance ($ Thousands)

Item	1965	1964	1963	1962	1961
Operating Data					
Net sales	$13,099	$ 8,042	$ 3,486	$ 475	$ —
Net income					
Before taxes	2,481	1,962	454	(694)	(314)
After taxes	1,331	1,002	218	(694)	(314)
Per common share	1.35	1.04	0.23	(0.85)	(0.42)
Depreciation	423	252	141	93	28
Research and					
development	747	452	288	457	308
Financial Data					
Working capital	1,977	994	642	331	586
Total assets	9,600	5,377	2,089	1,710	1,363
Long-term debt	2,352	1,037	—	—	—
Shareholders' equity	3,909	2,565	1,694	1,515	1,253

A SHIFT IN STRATEGY AND MANAGEMENT
APPROACH: 1965–1967

Whereas Memorex's early years had been marked by a closely knit top management group that dedicated itself to success in a single line of products, the period from 1965 to 1967 was one in which Memorex shifted its attention to managing a portfolio of diverse businesses. To do so, Laurence Spitters decided to skew sharply the allocation of both capital and incentives to his businesses depending on their growth potential. Spitters' approach, which was consistent with use of the portfolio approach to allocate resources, posed numerous administrative issues and problems.

Statement of Objectives

The blueprint for both the development and the management of Memorex's portfolio of businesses was explicitly articulated in November 1966, when Laurence Spitters circulated a 31-page statement of objectives to his 45 top managers. Although Spitters asked for comments on his statement of objectives, it is important to note that he had developed the statement on his own. In terms of his management approach, Spitters was shifting from managing the processes that produce strategies to directly managing outcomes.

The statement of objectives laid out Spitters' plan for Memorex until 1970. It began by stating that "the special emphasis of Memorex's operations is growth."[3] For Spitters, this meant not only the expansion of Memorex's tape business at the rate of 25% per year, but entry into three new businesses* that would generate $40 million of additional volume by 1970. In total, Memorex's sales were planned to increase to over $100 million by 1970. Table 11.2 details the sales objectives.

The decision to pursue three new businesses represented a

---

*The three new businesses were disk substrates, disk packs, and disk drives.

TABLE 11.2. FIVE-YEAR SALES OBJECTIVES OF MEMOREX CORPORATION ($ Million)

	Tape Operations			Nontape Operations				
Year	U.S.	International	Sales Tape Subtotal	Disk Substrates	Disk Packs	Disk Drives	Sales Nontape Subtotal	Total Memorex Sales
1966	$22	$ 4	$26	$1.5	—	—	$ 1.5	$ 27.5
1967	30	8	38	2.7	$2.5	—	5.2	43.2
1968	39	10	49	4.0	8.0	$5.0	17.0	66.0
1969	47	12	59	5.0	13.0	10.0	28.0	87.0
1970	53	14	67	5.0	20.0	15.0	40.0	107.0

choice to run Memorex as a portfolio of businesses rather than as a single-product tape company. For Spitters, it also meant that resources would be funneled from the tape business to support the three new businesses. In his statement of objectives, Spitters explained why it made sense to treat the tape business as a cash cow that would fund new business:

> U.S. tape operations and, to a great extent, European tape operations will face declining profit margins as the tape industry engenders the competitive conditions of a mature industry. Reduced profit margins may be countered periodically by new product improvements which do not represent technological breakthroughs, but these will not change the long-term results.
>
> Net profits from operations of Disk Pack Corporation and Peripheral Systems Corporation, given their success, should be better than those of the tape business because they will be the initial profits from successful operations.

While Spitters' decisions to enter new businesses and to manage Memorex as a portfolio of businesses may have had considerable merit, what was more significant was the way in which Spitters managed the portfolio of businesses.

Management Approach

Spitters' approach to achieving the growth that would be needed to offset the expected declines in the tape business was to offer tremendous incentives to the high-growth divisions and to select managers for the growth businesses who were highly entrepreneurial. The similarity between Spitters' approach and typical descriptions of how to apply the portfolio approach is striking.

To manage his growth businesses, Laurence Spitters sought out managers that he referred to as "wild ducks." He commented:

> It was my experience that there are two worlds of people, some of whom are very secure and comfortable and satisfied in their career pursuits in large institutionalized companies, and others of whom

are, I think, *wild ducks, and who are interested in perhaps greater challenges that small companies present in terms of the necessity to succeed or die.*

In many work environments, the constraints placed upon the individual by the nature of the institution are such as to sometimes make people uncomfortable.

The decision-making process is long and involved, sometimes not known, in the sense that the people who act upon decisions are not in close proximity to those who benefit or suffer from the effects of those decisions.

The formalization of the decision-making process is frequently an irritant, and for people who are unusually energetic and demanding, in the sense of desiring, themselves, to take action and to have their actions complemented by the actions of other people upon whom they are dependent, I would characterize these people as perhaps being wild ducks rather than tame ducks. In that sense, I wanted more "wild ducks" in our company.[4]

To attract and reward "wild ducks," Spitters organized the growth businesses into what he called entrepreneurial subsidiaries. An entrepreneurial subsidiary would have 80% of its stock owned by Memorex. The other 20% of its stock would be sold to the management of the subsidiary at approximately $1 per share. If the subsidiary created a product that was successful or met the criteria that Memorex set for its stock conversion, then the wild ducks would be given one share of Memorex stock for every one share of their stock in the entrepreneurial venture. For example, if a manager were offered 10,000 shares for $10,000 and was allowed to convert his stock to Memorex stock, which was selling at $50, that person's shares would be worth $500,000.

Needless to say, the entrepreneurial subsidiaries provided considerable incentive to get people focused on new product development and growth. In 1965 and 1966, three entrepreneurial subsidiaries were established—Disk Pack Corporation, Substrate Corporation, and Peripheral Systems Corporation—which developed the products for Memorex to enter the disk pack, disk platter, and disk drive businesses. All three were merged into

Memorex by 1967, providing substantial rewards to those who had worked at the entrepreneurial subsidiaries. For example, one of the employees who had helped establish Peripheral Systems Corporation (disk drives) had invested $12,000 in the stock of the subsidiary. When this stock was converted to Memorex shares, the Memorex shares were worth $1.4 million.

In establishing entrepreneurial subsidiaries, as with writing the statement of objectives, Laurence Spitters adopted a management approach wherein he directly managed outcomes and paid little attention to administrative constraints. He made these decisions himself and ignored the warnings of many of his top managers who did not support his plans.* For example, the responses Spitters received to his statement of objectives were overwhelmingly negative. While most of the responses did not take issue with Spitters' strategy of emphasizing growth and developing new businesses, they did criticize the imbalanced allocation of both resources and rewards to the entrepreneurial subsidiaries. The following excerpt from the response of W. L. Noon, a co-founder of Memorex, is typical:

> There can be really no question that magnetic tape profitability per unit will tend to decline in the forthcoming years and that substantial technical and managerial effort will be required to increase plant yields and efficiency, reduce working capital requirements and improve return on capital invested.
>
> It is particularly important for these reasons that the Disk Pack Corporation succeed. . . .
>
> Quite obviously I personally feel that Memorex is making a critically serious error in the decisions which are postulated herein. . . . **The Memorex tape division is conspicuous by its absence from consideration as a separate profit center with the same type of management incentive that has been provided for the Disk Pack, Perhipheral Systems and postulated European operations.** . . . If, as you say, entrepreneurial managers perform best when objectives are set, resources provided and operations are left unfettered

---

*It should be noted that the establishment of each entrepreneurial subsidiary did require board approval. But even at that level, there were abstentions.

in the Disk Pack and other postulated subsidiaries, it would appear to me to be equally true in the magnetic tape area. I believe that, whereas Memorex is striving to produce creative environments in its new subsidiaries, it is in fact striving to produce exactly the opposite in its parent corporation.[5] [emphasis added]

Noon's comments were echoed in virtually all of the written responses that Spitters received. For example, the vice president of sales, E. S. Seaman, wrote:

I feel that management discord is undoubtedly the biggest problem facing us today. We will never reach the one hundred million dollar mark without establishing a greater degree of harmony. Our company operates as four independent companies under one roof. This is an impossible situation. . . .

*It is also my opinion that **the Disk Pack Corporation must be carefully monitored by Memorex.**[6] [emphasis added]*

Despite clear indications of disagreement from his managers, who warned him that his approach to managing Memorex's portfolio could run the risks of not providing enough incentive to the computer tape business and not providing enough control of the new businesses, Laurence Spitters proceeded with his plans. The questionable nature of this choice can be better understood by examining all the forces that shape the processes of strategy formulation and implementation.

As shown in Table 11.3, two of the forces, the prescribed approach to portfolio implementation and the CEO agenda and management approach, suggested that Spitters proceed with his plans and management approach. But the other two forces, Memorex's financial resource position and administrative considerations, suggested that Spitters modify his approach. Administrative considerations, such as the impact of not providing incentives to the tape business and dissension within the top management group, suggested that Spitters should modify his approach. In terms of financial resources, Memorex's balance sheet was strong in the mid 1960s and, with its stock consistently selling at more than 30 times earnings, the company had access to

TABLE 11.3. FORCES SHAPING STRATEGY FORMULATION AND
IMPLEMENTATION IN THE MEMOREX CORPORATION

Portfolio and Strategic Analysis

Differentiate resource allocation
between divisions

*Administrative
Considerations*

Top managers disagree
with CEO's objectives
Few incentives for cash
cow business
Resentment by cash cow
business
Difficulty in controlling
growth businesses

*Formulation and Implementation
of Strategy*

Resources allocated to new
businesses, entrepreneurial
subsidiaries
Magnetic tape business
regarded as cash cow

*Agenda and Strategic
Management Mode of CEO*

Agenda to grow rapidly
via new businesses
Management of substance
rather than process
Ignoring of administrative
considerations

Financial Resources Position

Company strong financially
High stock multiple

equity capital. From a financial perspective, it was not necessary to cut off funding to the tape business because of a lack of financial resources. The fact that Laurence Spitters did not modify his management approach to account for all of the forces that shape strategy was probably a mistake on his part.

ADMINISTRATIVE ISSUES AND PROBLEMS: 1967–1971

Between 1967 and 1971, 20 additional entrepreneurial subsidiaries were started, each offering tremendous incentives to their founders. As these subsidiaries were merged into Memorex, giving their managers tremendous financial rewards, the administrative consequences of such sharply skewed incentives became apparent.

The first consequence had to do with the considerable leeway the subsidiary managers were given in the operation of the growth businesses. Although this was supposed to encourage creativity within the subsidiaries, the lack of top management control, along with steep incentives to develop products, often meant that operating problems within the subsidiaries were allowed to go uncorrected. Examples of operating problems that Memorex encountered with its entrepreneurial subsidiaries were development slippages, introduction of new products that still had bugs in them, and a lack of spare parts. These problems were often exacerbated after a subsidiary was merged into Memorex's existing businesses. It was often difficult to get the highly rewarded growth-business managers to cooperate with other units within the company, and many of them left the company after receiving their financial rewards. Thus Memorex's attempt to provide steep incentives and plentiful resources to its growth businesses led to numerous operating and administrative problems in those businesses.

Equally serious was the impact on Memorex's cash cow, the

magnetic tape business. The rewards given to the growth businesses were bound to cause resentment among employees in the tape business, none of whom were being offered such handsome rewards. In addition, with virtually all resources and rewards being directed to the growth businesses, the magnetic tape business was seriously neglected and many key employees chose to leave the company. Indeed all of the managers who had complained about Spitters' statement of objectives in 1966 left the company within the next few years. These were the same managers who had built and developed the tape business. As a result, by 1968 competitors were offering superior magnetic tape products. Memorex was very slow to match these competitive offerings, because of the lack of resources devoted to tape products. By the fourth quarter of 1970, Memorex's tape operations were experiencing losses: sales of computer tape in 1970 were only $34 million, about one half of the $67 million that Laurence Spitters had forecast in his earlier statement of objectives.

Financial Results

Memorex's financial performance between 1965 and 1971 is highlighted in Table 11.4. Although 1970 sales fell short of the $100 million objective, 1971 sales of $110 million exceeded the objective. But the sales figures mask the profit problems Memorex was experiencing. Through 1967, profit growth closely tracked sales growth. In 1968 and 1969, the entire increases in profit could be accounted for by the dubious accounting practice of capitalizing research and development expenditures. By 1970, profits declined by 55% and would have been negative had it not been for the deferral of over $8 million of research and development expenditures. And in 1971, for the first time since 1962 Memorex sustained a loss. Indeed the total of the 1971 loss of $13.4 million and the deferred R & D expense of $11.8 million exceeded the entire profit that Memorex had earned during the previous six years.

TABLE 11.4. FINANCIAL PERFORMANCE OF MEMOREX CORPORATION, 1965–1971

Item	Performance ($ Thousands)						
	1971	1970	1969	1968	1967	1966	1965
Operating Data							
Net sales and revenues	$ 110,201	$ 78,997	$ 74,067	$ 52,961	$ 33,957	$ 24,417	$ 13,099
Net income	(13,390)	3,183	6,902	4,939	3,576	2,724	1,331
Earnings per common share	(3.43)	0.83	1.85	1.34	1.06	0.89	0.45
Depreciation and amortization expense	26,984	11,314	5,860	3,476	1,687	828	423
Research and Development Expenditures							
Expenses against net sales and revenues during the year (including amortization)	5,096	4,824	5,141	3,458	2,361	1,454	747
Capitalized as cost of equipment for lease to others (including amortization)	9,814	3,177	403	360	16	—	—
Subtotal: Expenses and capitalized costs relating to products marketed	14,910	8,001	5,544	3,818	2,377	1,454	747
Capitalized as deferred research and development costs	11,840	8,141	3,683	1,487	758	178	—
Less: Amortization of deferred research and development costs	(6,341)	(1,577)	(387)	(134)	—	—	—
Total research and development expenditures	20,409	14,565	8,840	5,171	3,135	1,632	747
Financial Position							
Working capital	35,123	35,355	16,127	7,538	7,232	8,738	1,977
Total assets	318,129	223,655	88,197	52,988	30,981	24,156	9,600
Long-term debt:							
ILC Peripherals Leasing Corporation	89,718	31,628					
Memorex Corporation and majority-owned subsidiaries							
Bank credit and unsubordinated debt	65,146	26,873	22,354	4,285	—	55	2,352
Convertible subordinated debentures	75,000	75,040	65	4	6,816	12,000	—
Shareholders' equity	25,956	39,116	35,074	27,295	15,486	6,673	3,909

CONCLUSION

Memorex's poor financial performance in 1971 and the subsequent disastrous results in 1973 (a loss of $119 million) have been the subject of many interpretations and explanations.[7] Here, however, our purpose is not to sort out the many causes of Memorex's misfortunes but rather to identify some of the administrative issues that can arise from a sharply skewed allocation of resources and rewards to a company's portfolio of businesses.

Two sets of administrative issues arose at Memorex, one set dealing with the growth businesses and the other with the mature businesses. For Memorex's growth businesses, it was not enough only to offer steep incentives and plentiful resources. The administrative consequences were to make it difficult for top management to exert control over the growth businesses, to integrate them with the rest of the company, and to retain their managers. For the mature or cash cow businesses, the lack of resources brought resentment, low morale, resignations, and a loss of market leadership.

Interestingly, in a memo written in 1973, shortly before his resignation as CEO, Laurence Spitters acknowledged both sets of problems:

> The skew of the application of manpower and capital resources to the equipment business occurs without a comparative evaluation of the other, nonequipment business. . . .
>
> Corporate management, which is responsible to shareholders, creditors, and the general employment of Memorex, is unable to effect the direction or determine the results/objectives of operating management or to communicate effectively with operating management. Operating management is unresponsive to corporate control. Communications between management and within management organizations is seriously deficient.
>
> The media business [magnetic tape] also suffers from the problems of the integration, as follows.
>
> The domestic field sales organization has been decimated. . . .

Reduction of media technical staff has also eliminated some essential technical talent required to develop improved processes and products.

The media business had no "identity" to which employees of the several functions can relate; their sense is that the results of the media business are not measured and rewarded and that its future is unplanned.[8]

Whereas the General Electric Company and the Dexter Corporation modified their use of portfolio planning techniques to account for administrative consequences, the Memorex Corporation did not. To some extent, this difference may be due to the fact that Memorex's experiences are confined to an earlier period. But whatever the reason, Memorex's experiences have aided this research by providing an unencumbered view of the administrative issues posed by the sharp skewing of resource allocation and incentives that is often associated with the portfolio approach. And when considered together, the three cases point to the necessity of the CEO's modifying the portfolio approach not only to serve specific purposes but also to maintain consistency with the company's financial condition and administrative constraints.

NOTES

CHAPTER 1

[1]Fred Borch's discussion with his senior executives was tape recorded and a transcript was prepared. The transcript was made available to me by the General Electric Company.

[2]For a popular critique, see: "The New Breed of Strategic Planner," *Business Week* (September 17, 1984): 62–68.

[3]Phillippe Haspeslagh, "Portfolio Planning: Uses and Limits," *Harvard Business Review* (January–February 1982): 58–74.

[4]Robert H. Hayes and William J. Abernathy, "Managing Our Way to Economic Decline," *Harvard Business Review* (July–August 1980): 67–77.

[5]For a review of the debate about the theory underlying portfolio planning, see: Stuart St. P. Slatter, "Common Pitfalls in Using the BCG Product Portfolio Matrix," *London School of Business Journal* (Winter 1980): 18–22; Michael Lubatkin and Michael Pitts, "PIMS: Fact or Folklore," *The Journal of Business Strategy* (Winter 1983): 38–43; George S. Day, "Diagnosing the Product Portfolio," *Journal of Marketing* (April 1977): 29–38.

[6]Yoram Wind and Vijay Mahajan, "Designing Product and Business Portfolios," *Harvard Business Review* (January–February 1981): 155–165.

[7]Yoram Wind, Vijay Mahajan, and Donald J. Swire, "An Empirical Comparison of Standardized Portfolio Models," *Journal of Marketing* (Spring 1983): 89–99.

[8]Richard A. Bettis and William K. Hall, "Strategic Portfolio Management in the Multibusiness Firm," *California Management Review* (Fall 1981): 23–38.

[9]Winfred B. Hirschman, "Profit from the Learning Curve," *Harvard Business Review* (January–February 1964): 125–139.

[10]For more background on experience curves, see: Boston Consulting Group, "Perspectives on Experience," Boston Consulting Group, Inc., 1972; Arnoldo C.

Hax and Nicolas S. Majluf, "Competitive Cost Dynamics: The Experience Curve," *Interfaces* (October 1982): 50–61.

[11]For a more detailed description of the growth–share matrix, see: Boston Consulting Group, "The Product Portfolio Concept," Perspective No. 66, Boston Consulting Group, Inc., 1970; Boston Consulting Group, "The Experience Curve Reviewed—The Concept," Perspective No. 124, Boston Consulting Group, Inc., 1970; Boston Consulting Group, "The Experience Curve Reviewed—The Growth Share Matrix of the Product Portfolio," Perspective No. 135, Boston Consulting Group, Inc., 1973; Arnoldo C. Hax and Nicolas S. Majluf, "The Use of the Growth–Share Matrix in Strategic Planning," *Interfaces* (October 1982): 50–61.

[12]For a more detailed description of the company position–industry attractiveness screen, see: William E. Rothschild, *Putting it all Together: A Guide to Strategic Thinking* (New York: AMACOM, 1976); Arnoldo C. Hax and Nicolas S. Majluf, "The Use of the Industry Attractiveness-Business Strength Matrix in Strategic Planning," *Interfaces* (April 1983): 54–71.

[13]For a more detailed description of the PIMS approach, see: Robert D. Buzzell, Bradley T. Gale, and Ralph G. M. Sultan, "Market Share—A Key to Profitability," *Harvard Business Review* (January–February 1975): 97.

[14]William J. Abernathy and Kenneth Wayne, "Limits of the Learning Curve," *Harvard Business Review* (September–October 1974): 109–119; William E. Fruhan, Jr., "Pyrrhic Victories in Fights for Market Share," *Harvard Business Review* (September–October 1972): 100–107; Hax and Majluf, "Competitive Cost Dynamics: The Experience Curve".

[15]Richard P. Rumelt, *Strategy, Structure, and Economic Performance* (Boston: Division of Research, Graduate School of Business Administration, Harvard University, 1974).

[16]Joseph L. Bower, *Managing the Resource Allocation Process: A Study of Corporate Planning and Investment* (Boston: Division of Research, Graduate School of Business Administration, Harvard University, 1970).

[17]Bower, *Managing the Resource Allocation Process*.

[18]Alfred D. Chandler, Jr., *The Visible Hand: The Managerial Revolution in American Business* (Cambridge, Mass.: The Belknap Press of the Harvard University Press, 1977).

[19]Phillippe C. Haspeslagh, "Portfolio Planning Approaches and the Strategic Management Process in Diversified Industrial Companies" (DBA dissertation, Harvard University, Graduate School of Business Administration, 1983).

[20]Roderick Edward White, "Structural Context, Strategy and Performance" (DBA dissertation, Harvard University, Graduate School of Business Administration, 1981).

[21]Bruce D. Henderson, *Henderson on Corporate Strategy* (Cambridge, Mass.: Abt Books, 1979).

[22]Hayes and Abernathy, "Managing Our Way to Economic Decline."

[23]As quoted in Imperial Corporation (A), Harvard Business School Case #9-380-123, prepared by Norman A. Berg.

[24]Walter Kiechel III, "The Decline of The Experience Curve," *Fortune* (October 5, 1981): 139–146; Walter Kiechel III, "Three (or Four, or More) Ways to Win," *Fortune* (October 19, 1981): 181–188; Walter Kiechel III, "Oh Where, Oh Where Has My Little Dog Gone? Or My Cash Cow? Or My Star?" *Fortune* (November 2, 1981): 148–154; Walter Kiechel III, "Playing the Global Game," *Fortune* (November 16, 1981): 111–126.

[25]Walter Kiechel III, "Corporate Strategists Under Fire," *Fortune* (December 27, 1982): 34–39.

CHAPTER 2

[1]The Norton example is described in detail in "Norton Company: Strategic Planning for Diversified Operations," Harvard Business School Case #9-380-003, prepared by Professor Francis Aguilar.

[2]For a full description of the relationship between financial goals and strategy, see Gordon Donaldson and Jay W. Lorsch, *Decision Making at the Top* (New York: Basic Books, 1983), Ch. 4:49–78.

[3]Kenneth R. Andrews, *The Concept of Corporate Strategy* (Homewood, Ill.: Richard D. Irwin, 1980): 18.

[4]Igor Ansoff, "The Changing Shape of the Strategy Problem," in Dan E. Schendel and Charles W. Hofer, Eds., *Strategic Management* (Boston: Little, Brown, 1979); Charles W. Hofer and Dan Schendel, *Strategy Formulation: Analytical Concepts* (St. Paul: West Publishing, 1978); Peter Lorange, *Corporate Planning* (Englewood Cliffs, N. J.: Prentice-Hall, 1980).

[5]Andrews, *The Concept of Corporate Strategy*. Andrews also makes an important distinction between economic strategy and ethical and value considerations. Unfortunately, most of the recent work in policy has ignored this distinction or defined new variables, that is, culture or shared values, that are implied in Andrews' concept. I chose the term *institutional strategy* to emphasize that basic character, values, and vision are all part of a company's total strategy.

[6]Andrews, *The Concept of Corporate Strategy*.

[7]Gil Burck, "International Business Machines," *Fortune* (January, 1940): 36–40.

[8]"IBM's Basic Beliefs," *IBM Orientation Booklet*, undated.

[9]Donaldson and Lorsch, *Decision Making at the Top*.

[10]"The Lincoln Electric Company," Harvard Business School Case #9-376-02, prepared by Norman A. Berg.

[11]Terrence E. Deal and Allan A. Kennedy, *Corporate Cultures* (Reading, Mass.: Addison-Wesley, 1982): 4.

[12]Frederick W. Gluck, "Vision and Leadership in Corporate Strategy," *The McKinsey Quarterly* (Winter 1981): 13–27.

[13]Thomas J. Peters, "Organizing for the '80's: Farewell to Gimmicks . . . Back to Basics or 'Keep it Simple, Stupid'," keynote speech, The Intersection of Organization Development and Management Consulting—Opportunities for Synergy Conference (April 30, 1980).

[14]Richard Tanner Pascale and Anthony G. Athos, *The Art of Japanese Management* (New York: Simon and Schuster, 1981); Thomas J. Peters and Robert H. Waterman, Jr., *In Search of Excellence* (New York, Harper & Row, 1982); Donaldson and Lorsch, *Decision Making at the Top.*

[15]Ken Auletta, "A Certain Poetry—Parts I and II," *The New Yorker* (June 6, 1983, and June 13, 1983): 50–91.

[16]Henry Mintzberg, "Patterns in Strategy Formation," *Management Science* 24, No. 9 (May 1978): 934–948; Robert A. Burgleman, "A Model of the Interaction of Strategic Behavior, Corporate Context, and the Concept of Strategy," *Academy of Management Review* 3, No. 1 (1983): 61–70.

[17]Henry Mintzberg, "Strategy Making in Three Modes," *California Management Review,* Vol. XVI, No. 2 (Winter 1973): 44–53.

[18]"A Note on Implementing Strategy," Harvard Business School Case #9-383-015, prepared by Richard G. Hamermesh.

[19]This example is excerpted from John M. Hobbs and Donald F. Heany, "Coupling Strategy to Operating Plans," *Harvard Business Review* (May–June 1977): 119–126.

[20]This is far from a trivial task. For a complete treatment, see Malcolm S. Salter and Wolf A. Weinhold, *Diversification Through Acquisition* (New York: The Free Press, 1979).

[21]Deal and Kennedy, *Corporate Cultures;* Pascale and Athos, *The Art of Japanese Management;* Peters and Waterman, *In Search of Excellence.*

[22]Thomas J. Peters, Leadership issue of *Executive* (1980).

[23]For descriptions of the strategic process, see: Joseph L. Bower, "Planning Within the Firm," *Journal of the American Economic Association* (May 1970): 186–194; Donaldson and Lorsch, *Decision Making at the Top;* Mintzberg, "Patterns in Strategy Formulation"; James Brian Quinn, *Strategies for Change: Logical Incrementalism* (Homewood, Ill.: Richard D. Irwin, 1980).

[24]Quinn, *Strategies for Change: Logical Incrementalism,* pp. 87–88.

CHAPTER 3

[1]Gordon Donaldson and Jay W. Lorsch, *Decision Making at the Top* (New York: Basic Books, 1983).

[2]Kenneth R. Andrews, *The Concept of Corporate Strategy* (Homewood, Ill.: Richard D. Irwin, 1980): 27.

[3]Richard M. Cyert and James G. March, *A Behavioral Theory of the Firm* (Englewood Cliffs, New Jersey: Prentice-Hall, 1963). Charles E. Lindblom, "The Science of 'Muddling Through'," *Public Administration Review*, (Spring 1959): 79−88.

[4]Joseph L. Bower, *Managing the Resource Allocation Process* (Division of Research, Graduate School of Business Administration, Harvard University, 1970): 305.

[5]James Brian Quinn, *Strategies for Change: Logical Incrementalism*, (Homewood, Ill.: Richard D. Irwin, 1980): 51.

[6]Donaldson and Lorsch, *Decision Making at the Top*; Richard R. Ellsworth, "Corporate Strategy and Capital Structure Policies: A Descriptive Study," (DBA dissertation, Graduate School of Business Administration, Harvard University, 1980).

[7]Donaldson and Lorsch, *Decision Making at the Top*, p. 72.

[8]Donaldson and Lorsch, *Decision Making at the Top*; Richard R. Ellsworth, "Subordinate Financial Policy to Corporate Strategy," *Harvard Business Review*, 61, No. 6 (November−December 1983): 170−182.

[9]Abraham Zaleznick, "Managers and Leaders: Are They Different?" *Harvard Business Review*, 55, No. 3 (May−June 1977): 67−78.

[10]For a discussion of the limited power of chief executives, see: Cyert and March, *A Behavioral Theory of the Firm*, or Jeffrey Pfeffer and Gerald R. Salancik, *The External Control of Organizations: A Resource Dependence Perspective* (New York: Harper & Row, 1978).

[11]H. Edward Wrapp, "Good Managers Don't Make Policy Decisions," *Harvard Business Review*, 45, No. 5 (September−October 1967): 1−99.

[12]John P. Kotter, *The General Managers* (New York: The Free Press, 1982).

[13]James N. Kelly, "Management Transitions for Newly Appointed CEO's," *Sloan Management Review*, 22, No. 1 (Fall 1980): 37−45. John J. Gabarro, "The Development of Trust, Influence, and Expectations," in Anthony G. Athos and John J. Gabarro, Eds., *Interpersonal Behavior* (Englewood Cliffs, N.J.: Prentice Hall, 1978).

[14]Kelly, "Management Transitions for Newly Appointed CEO's," p. 45.

[15]Kotter, *The General Managers*.

CHAPTER 4

[1]"The Mead Corporation," Harvard Business School Case #9-379-070, prepared by Professor Francis J. Aguilar.

[2]These remarks were taken from the management presentation to Paper and Forest Products analysts on February 8, 1977, by James McSwiney, William Wommack, and Warren Batts, New York.

[3]S. Clark Gilmour, "The Divestment Decision Process" (DBA dissertation, Harvard University, Graduate School of Business Administration, 1973).

[4]Geoffrey Smith, "Culture Shift," *Forbes* (October 24, 1983): 69.

[5]For an excellent review of the literature on corporate acquisitions, see: Michael Bradley, Anand Desai, and E. Han Kim, "Determinants of the Wealth Effects of Corporate Acquisition: Theory and Evidence" (Working Paper, University of Michigan, Graduate School of Business Administration, September 1983).

[6]Bendix Annual Report 1980: 3; Bendix Annual Report 1981: 6.

[7]General Electric Annual Report 1973.

[8]General Electric Annual Report 1976.

[9]"Allied Corporation (A)," "Allied Corporation (B)," Harvard Business School Case #9-383-076 and #9-383-078, prepared by Richard E. Ellsworth.

[10]For more information on Haspeslagh's questionnaire, see: Philippe C. Haspeslagh, "Portfolio Planning: Uses and Limits," *Harvard Business Review* (January–February 1982): 58–74; Philippe C. Haspeslagh, "Portfolio Planning Approaches and the Strategic Management Process in Diversified Industrial Companies," (DBA dissertation, Harvard University, Graduate School of Business Administration, 1983).

CHAPTER 5

[1]Derek F. Abell, *Defining the Business: The Starting Point of Strategic Planning* (Englewood Cliffs, N. J.: Prentice-Hall, 1980).

[2]All of the quotations of Mr. Borch came from a transcript of comments he made to General Electric corporate officers at a meeting on May 14, 1970. The transcript was made available by the General Electric Company.

[3]Philippe Haspeslagh, "Portfolio Planning Approaches and the Strategic Management Process in Diversified Industrial Companies" (DBA dissertation, Harvard University, Graduate School of Business Administration, 1983).

[4]Haspeslagh, "Portfolio Planning."

[5]Haspeslagh, "Portfolio Planning."

[6]Charles G. Burck, "Will Success Spoil General Motors," *Fortune* (August 22, 1983): 95–104; Anne B. Fisher, "GM's Unlikely Revolutionist," *Fortune* (March 9, 1984): 106–112.

[7]Robert A. Burgelman, "A Model of the Interaction of Strategic Behavior, Corporate Context, and the Concept of Strategy," *Academy of Management Review* 8, No. 1: 67.

[8]Abell, *Defining the Business: The Starting Point of Strategic Planning*, p. 5.

CHAPTER 6

[1]Alfred P. Sloan, Jr., *My Years with General Motors* (Garden City, N. Y.: Doubleday, 1972): 58.

[2]Richard F. Vancil, *Decentralization: Managerial Ambiguity by Design* (Homewood, Ill.: Dow Jones-Irwin, 1978): 3.

[3]Myron Magnet, "Timex Takes the Torture Test," *Fortune* (June 27, 1983): 112–115, 118, 120.

[4]For a discussion of problems of managing rapid growth, see: John P. Kotter and Vijay Sathe, "Problems of Human Resource Management in Rapidly Growing Companies," *California Management Review* (Winter 1978), Vol. 21, No. 2: 29–36; Heywood Klein, "Zooming Firms of 1980 Find That Fast Growth Can Turn Into a Curse," *The Wall Street Journal* (August 24, 1983): 1.

[5]Research about acquisitions suggests that the high price paid has a negative effect on the performance of the acquiring company. See: Michael Bradley, Anand Desai, and E. Han Kim, "Determinants of the Wealth Effects of Corporate Acquisition: Theory and Evidence" (Working Paper, The University of Michigan, Graduate School of Business Administration, September 1983).

[6]Philippe Haspeslagh, "Portfolio Planning Approaches and the Strategic Management Process in Diversified Industrial Companies" (DBA dissertation, Harvard University, Graduate School of Business Administration, 1983).

[7]Roderick Edward White, "Structural Context, Strategy and Performance" (DBA dissertation, Harvard University, Graduate School of Business Administration, 1981); Richard G. Hamermesh and Roderick E. White, "Manage Beyond Portfolio Analysis," *Harvard Business Review*, 62, No. 1 (January–February 1984): 103–109.

[8]White, "Structural Context."

CHAPTER 7

[1]Richard G. Hamermesh, M. J. Anderson, Jr., and J. E. Harris, "Strategies for Low Market Share Businesses," *Harvard Business Review*, 56, No. 3 (May–June 1978): 95–102. Carolyn Y. Woo and Arnold C. Cooper, "The Surprising Case for Low Market Share," *Harvard Business Review*, 60, No. 6 (November–December 1982): 106–113. Richard G. Hamermesh and Steven B. Silk, "How to Compete in Stagnant Industries," *Harvard Business Review*, 57, No. 5 (September–October 1979): 161–168.

[2]Michael E. Porter, *Competitive Strategy: Techniques for Analyzing Industries and Competitors* (New York: The Free Press, 1980).

[3]Porter, *Competitive Strategy*; William K. Hall, "Survival Strategies in a Hostile Environment," *Harvard Business Review* (September–October 1980); Michael E. Porter, *Competitive Advantage* (New York: The Free Press, 1984).

[4]S. Clark Gilmour, "The Divestment Decision Process" (DBA dissertation, Harvard University Graduate School of Business Administration, 1973).

[5]Philippe C. Haspeslagh, "Portfolio Planning Approaches and Strategic Management Process in Diversified Industrial Companies" (DBA dissertation, Harvard University Graduate School of Business Administration, 1983).

[6]Haspeslagh, "Portfolio Planning."

[7]Malcolm S. Salter and Wolf A. Weinhold, "Merger Trends and Prospects for the 1980s," U. S. Department of Commerce, December 1980.

[8]Robert Hayes, "Strategic Planning: Forward in Reverse?" Draft, Harvard Business School, December 1984.

[9]The contrast between companies that behave as if they are resource constrained, rather than opportunity driven, was first articulated by Howard Stevenson. See: Howard H. Stevenson, and David E. Gumpert, "The Heart of Entrepreneurship," *Harvard Business Review*, 63, No. 2, (March–April 1985): 85–94.

[10]Thomas J. Peters, "Organizing for the '80s: Farewell to Gimmicks . . . Back to Basics or 'Keep it Simple, Stupid' "(keynote speech, The Intersection of Organization Development and Management Consulting—Opportunities for Synergy Conference, April 30, 1980).

[11]Richard Tanner Pascale and Anthony G. Athos, *The Art of Japanese Management* (New York: Simon and Schuster, 1981).

[12]Haspeslagh, "Portfolio Planning."

[13]Salter and Weinhold, "Merger Trends."

[14]Salter and Weinhold, "Merger Trends," p. 37.

[15]To illustrate Perkin-Elmer's reputation for planning, consider that in 1980, *Dun's Business Monthly* selected Perkin-Elmer as one of the five best-managed companies in the United States. The title of the article was "Perkin-Elmer: The Persistent Planner."

CHAPTER 8

[1]Joseph L. Bower, "Restructuring Industry: A Problem for Contemporary Managements," paper prepared for use in the Harvard Business School 75th Anniversary Colloquium on United States Competition in the World Economy (February 13–16, 1984).

[2]Kenneth Andrews, "Corporate Strategy: The Essential Intangibles," remarks to the 1983 Strategic Planning Conference Board (New York, March 22, 1983): p. 5.

[3]Robert D. Buzzell, Bradley T. Gale, and Ralph G. M. Sultan, "Market Share—A Key to Profitability," *Harvard Business Review* (January–February 1975): 97–108.

[4]Robert S. Kaplan, "Yesterday's Accounting Undermines Production," *Harvard Business Review* (July–August 1984): 95–101.

[5]Thomas J. Peters and Robert H. Waterman, Jr., *In Search of Excellence: Lessons from America's Best-Run Companies* (New York: Harper & Row, 1982).

CHAPTER 9

[1]Worth Loomis, "Strategic Planning in Uncertain Times," *Chief Executive*, Vol. 14 (Winter 1980–81): 7–12.

CHAPTER 10

[1]Ann M. Morrison, "CEO's Pick the Best CEO's," *Fortune* (May 4, 1981): 133–136.

[2]The following accounts are typical: "Strategic Management in General Electric," *Operations Research* (November–December 1973): 1177–1182; "With 'Strategic Planning' GE Meets Land Mobile Challenges," *Communications* (April 1977): 26–32; "GE's Planned Prognosis," *Management Today* (August 1978): 66–69; "The Five Best Managed Companies," *Dun's Review* (December 1978): 29–44.

[3]James P., Baughman, "Problems and Performance of the Role of the Chief Executive in the General Electric Company, 1892–1974" (Mimeo, Boston: Division of Research, Graduate School of Business Administration, Harvard University, 1971).

[4]Fred Borch's discussion with his senior executives was tape recorded and a transcript was prepared. The transcript was made available to me by the General Electric Company.

[5]J. Thackray, "GE's Planned Prognosis," *Management Today* (August 1978): 66–69.

CHAPTER 11

[1]*Memorex v. IBM*, Testimony by L. L. Spitters, Trial Transcript: 6271–6272.

[2]Speech given by L. L. Spitters to the Industrial Management Club of San Jose and Santa Clara County, October 10, 1967.

[3]This quote and the ones that follow are excerpted from L. L. Spitters' Statement of Objectives, November 11, 1966. *Memorex v. IBM*, Defendant's Exhibit 32105.

[4]*U. S. v. IBM*, Testimony by L. L. Spitters, Trial Transcript: 42094–42096.

[5]*Memorex v. IBM*, Defendant's Exhibit 11045.

[6]*Memorex v. IBM*, Defendant's Exhibit 04231.

[7]The following accounts are typical: "Memorex: Reversing the Trend," *Datamation* (April 1972): 76; "Memorex Staggers from Another Wound," *Business Week* (February 10, 1973): 24−25; "Memorex Almost Killed Itself Diversifying," *Computerworld* (November 29, 1976): 50; "The Loneliness of the Master Turnaround Man," *Fortune* (February 1976): 110−128.

[8]*Memorex v. IBM*, Defendant's Exhibit 10592 A.

Index

241